Contents

Acknowledgements

First I want to thank my husband Jan for his love and ever-lasting support. Without him, I would not have been able to come this far and have this manual published. Jan, thank you and I love you!

Second I want to thank Dr. John Hanson for teaching me his techniques and how to use Tooties to help children develop. Through many years of observing thousands of children, he gained a lot of knowledge on how children develop and was able to help them improve in school. He was way ahead of his time when science emphasized that learning was purely a mental skill, processed in the brain only. Fortunately, more and more scientists are beginning to acknowledge what he has observed for a long time, that the body is very important in the mind-body learning process as well. Working together with behavioural optometrists Jerry Getman OD., and Homer H. Hendrickson OD., helped him to understand and develop the value of Tooties for vision training.

During my training, he stressed the importance of going through all the exercises, giving me many opportunities to learn how to learn as well. Through the years I have been able to better understand the various (learning) skills and how they can be seen in relation to the learning process, adding to the value of the Tooties teaching techniques.

Since English is not my native language, I owe Susan Huggen-berger a lot of gratitude for her advice, her knowledge and her dedication, as well as for spending many hours on editing the manuscripts. Conveying concepts in another language is not always easy, and because of her work this manual has become much more readable and understandable. Correcting and editing this manual has been very time consuming and we have spent many hours exchanging ideas on how to make the manual easier to understand for readers with various backgrounds. Her advice and support has been invaluable.

Nathalie Weytjens (Belgium) and Smita Trivedi (London, UK) have contributed their experience and knowledge as Behavioral Optometrists and I am indebted to them for the time they spent to contribute a chapter. As vision plays a very important role in developing learning skills their contributions are very valuable. As professionals in this field, they are more able to convey the importance of vision than I am.

Rosemarie Lechner, my Tooties teaching-colleague in Vienna, and Carola Koppermann have translated this manual into German with the kind help of Maria Spirik and Roswitha Weingartner, making the information more easily accessible to German-speaking professionals and parents. I owe them a lot of gratitude for their efforts as this has been a time consuming project for them. Without them the publication of the German manual would not have been possible.

Roswitha Weingartner has done much valuable work in Austria, training many teachers on how to help children, especially handicapped children, to develop their potential. Even though she has stepped back from active training activities she is still the 'mother of Tooties' in Austria.

Finally, but equally important, I want to thank everybody, who has supported me and shared ideas with me. I sincerely hope this manual will contribute to helping those many children who continue to experience difficulties in developing the way they should.

Thea van Eijk-Looijmans B.Ed
The Netherlands

Preface

Numerous children today show signs of delayed motor development parallel to a delay in speech and/or language development. When delayed motor abilities are built up and refined it has a direct impact on speech and language, as well as on a child's overall development. It is time to look at the 'whole child' and ask the necessary questions about why some children do what they do, behave as they do, and why some of them, who have an average intellect or above, have more difficulties than others to blossom and bloom at school.

Many of us in North America and Western Europe live under privileged circumstances, and many of us have slipped into comfortable but sedentary life styles. Somewhat exaggerated, we look straight ahead and move very little. Many children's motor and sensory systems develop slowly which influences their abilities and later performance in school. At home and in school settings delayed motor development (including delayed visual-motor development) is frequently not seen as a possible underlying component of developmental and school-related problems. But, motor development can play a part in speech and language development and subsequent school performance and it provides 'good performers' with that little extra edge. We live in a competitive world where people who have maintained these skills will have the advantage.

Life is movement, and movement, coupled with attention are the foundation of learning. The development of movement and vision is a mental process which cannot be separated and are fundamental to the development of speech and language. As you will read later, sight is what we see with our eyes and vision is the integrated understanding of all of the sensory input we receive and interpret with our body and minds. Vision is the mental interpretation of all our senses providing orientation and understanding with our brain. It is an external reflection of internal neurological organization. These concepts and many others were presented by Albert A. Sutton, OD, MS, FCOVD, at a recent workshop on Holistic Vision Care for Developmental/Learning Disabilities. How can motor development, balance, integration, and vision have anything to do with speech and language development?

Learning is not just taking in what the environment has to offer or a mental process alone but is coupled with the ability to skillfully use motor skills, as well as the ability to coordinate and use incoming and outgoing sensory impulses. A skilled motor foundation has to be developed in a positive atmosphere before learning can be successful. Parents and teachers may have a difficult time understanding that sometimes early gross motor skills need to be developed before their goals can be reached.

Eyes are complex and their functioning is a highly dynamic process which many parents and teachers may not realize. My own experience of a bicycle accident resulting in a significant injury to my head, and subsequent difficulties while reading (3 years later), made this very clear to me. You will read about visual skills and visual development in a later chapter. If there is a weakness or a delay in development it can affect how a child processes information with his eyes and affect language development and school performance, something which most teachers may not consider. Children with functional delays or weaknesses can present a variety of different behavioral patterns, such as poor eye contact, signs of distractibility, early fatigue, difficulty coloring in between lines, poor handwriting or poor eye-hand coordination, a lack of interest in reading, poor reading comprehension, apparent clumsiness, or avoidance of activities involving movement, just to name a few.

Continuing education courses have shown me that balance is an integral part of movement. A delay in development affects how we move our bodies and use our eyes, how we understand or interpret our senses, how vision and imagery develops, and how we use our minds and develop language. Movement and balance, which could be seen as active mental problem-solving, develops before concrete problem solving that children are faced with in school. Imagine moving a specific table from one room through a doorway and into the next room. What is quicker and more efficient, trial and error, or picturing the process in our mind? We picture things in our minds (objects, actions, as well as letters, words and numbers). Children begin picturing people and objects in their minds as language develops. As they grow and explore their pictures are refined. 'Seeing' is the process of visualizing and recognizing or interpreting what we see.

Our visual, as well as other sensory experiences, are saved in our memory and help us to understand, learn and make judgments. Consistent, reliable experiences and pictures contribute to an individual's knowledge. This knowledge accompanies each child to school, is expanded in school, and again, provides an important foundation. Some people's abilities to image or picture are highly developed, others are less refined, but they can be developed. Imagery and/or vision are an essential part of oral and written comprehension, language expression and thinking skills. Children learn these skills while doing, being involved in activities and talking about them. While moving we apply our skills to our daily lives. This applies to language development as well. Through repetition we learn to control and refine our knowledge and repetition verifies and solidifies what we know. Consider the importance this has on development and education.

Unfortunately we have begun to do a lot of things to disrupt and delay development. In some cases we nurture children to the point where they get more than everything they need and want without making an effort. Young children learn very early how to use crying to push the necessary buttons, especially in busy households, and most of the time it is very reliable.

We cannot problem-solve for our children. If we do, a child can grow up not being able to maintain the same pace as those who have learned this skill. We can learn to become better observers and to guide them. Our children have to learn by themselves by moving (active participation) and having the opportunity to apply developing skills. I am not advocating that we do not support our children, but rather, questioning our approach, looking at things from different points of view, and finding a healthy balance is important.

A pre-school evaluation by a Speech-Language Pathologist and an additional evaluation by a Functional or Behavioral Optometrist are highly recommended if a parent suspects visual-motor difficulties or a child is experiencing speech and/or language delays. Functional difficulty of eye performance is more common than most people realize and for parents and teachers it is not always obvious. Attention to overall development with the assistance of professional advice can help remediate or prevent delayed speech and language development or delayed motor development.

Taken one step further, it also affects school progress, or lack of it, related to delayed development. Tooties and the Tootie materials have been well thought through, planned and developed. The mindfulness of Functional Optometrists realized the value behind them and supplied input to help further develop them. Tooties attract children's attention, are wonderful to work with and have a high educational value if used in a thoughtful manner. Unless Tooties are used for feeling, counting, weighing or building roads, towers or structures, the body is constantly in motion and the eyes have a natural, fun, 3D opportunity to follow a moving object. This manual is based on experience and is packed full of very valuable information. It offers some wonderful activities and exercises to develop an individual's motor and visual abilities, as well as counting, math and thinking skills.

Change and growth frequently mean looking at and thinking about a situation from different perspectives, and it needs tremendous support from parents at home. Problem solving is often best done with help from different sources that work and cooperate together. Make an honest evaluation of each individual situation, as well as an honest look at intensions when determining what goals want and need to be reached. Weaknesses, if interfering with goals and progress, need to be remediated at the correct level. Have the courage to momentary reduce 'age relevant' expectations and develop the necessary early foundation skills first. Respect and acknowledge each child's tremendous efforts to develop delayed skills. Little steps are important goals to reach. They want to achieve success and do what other children can do as much as parents, if not more. If we can tap their inner energy and interest, half the 'battle' is already won. Make changes in a child's immediate surroundings to further support development. Arrange the environment and create the circumstances to support learning and the development of thinking skills. Children continually need opportunities to move and regain or strengthen abilities. Opportunities for repetition, as well as a positive, supportive attitude, are important to any learning success.

Susan Huggenberger-Jones, M.S.
Speech-Language Pathologist
Basel, Switzerland

Foreword

Jim King, O.D.

Have you heard about Tooties? I was asked that question about 40 years ago. Throughout the years, we have done a lot of research and picked the brains of a lot of interesting people. One of the most interesting was Dr. John Hanson—Dr. Tootie who developed Tooties to develop brain power.

Tooties are very versatile and can blend into therapy programs in a variety of ways. At a preschool level, Tooties can be sorted by color, texture, weight, fabric, and design. In addition to being thrown and caught, they can be stacked, launched, and bounced.

Tooties make it easy to observe the visual process as it is happening. When I do a visual therapy workup, one of the tests I give is a Tootie survey. I show them a Tootie Toss and say, "This is a Tootie Toss and this is a Tootie." I ask, "What do you think would happen if I tossed the Tootie at the Tootie Toss?" They ponder the alternatives. "It might go through a hole." "It could knock the Tootie Toss down." After they run out of ideas we try it and they see that the Tootie bounces back.

"Now, what do you think I'm going to ask you to do?" "Catch it?" "Exactly, but don't let it hit your nose!" As they throw the Tootie, we can watch: 1) Overall Posture, 2) Which hand do they choose, 3) Where are their feet positioned and which foot do they lead with?, 4) How do they catch? Right hand, left, or both? Do they reach out and get the Tootie or do they wait for the Tootie to come to them?

Children who throw with their right hand and right foot forward, or left hand with the left foot forward are moving in a homolateral pattern. When they throw with the right hand and lead with the left foot, or throw with the left hand and lead with the left foot, this is a cross pattern.

Those who move in a homolateral pattern are often out of balance and may even get hit in the nose when trying to catch. Fortunately, Tooties are soft and don't hurt. Those who move in a cross patterned manner are better balanced and more likely to catch the Tootie. In many cases the preferred cross pattern will emerge as the child has the opportunity to gain catching and throwing experience with the Tooties.

Catching Tooties is fun and helps develop a sense of accomplishment. "Let's see how many Tooties you can catch in a row?" Whatever number that is, we write that down. During each subsequent visual therapy session, we spend some "Tootie Time" and try to improve on their record. One of the characteristics of a strong therapy activity is the patient's chance to measure their own progress in a meaningful way. Keeping score adds to the fun and the child is motivated to improve on the record.

Dr. Tootie designed a Tootie launcher. It is a board with a fulcrum. A Tootie can be placed on one end and the child can stomp on the other end to launch the Tootie into the air. The Tootie launcher can be used to develop coordination between the eyes, hands, and feet as the child launches and catches the Tooties.

Introduce the child to the Tootie Launcher as follows: "This is a Tootie Launcher and the is a Tootie. How do you think we could use them together?" Wait for their response. 1) Some may use the Tootie Launcher as a teeter-tooter and throw the Tootie at the Tootie Toss from there. 2) Some may use it as a rocking rail. 3) Some use it as a bat to hit the Tootie. We encourage divergent thinking and creativity. If they do not discover it themselves, we guide them into the possibility of stomping on one end to launch the Tootie. The first successful launch is almost always marked by a sense of joy and accomplishment.

Once the ability to launch a single Tootie is mastered, two Tooties, or more can be launched. Use two different color Tooties. Place one at the far end of the launcher and the second somewhat closer to the middle. "If you launch both Tooties, which one do you think will go higher?" After some experimentation and practice, the child should discover that the Tooties position on the launcher determines which Tootie goes higher. This analysis is important as a child learns to catch the Tooties they launch. There is more time to catch the one that goes the highest.

"How many Tooties do you think you can launch and then catch at once?" Catching more than a few Tooties requires being able to stack the Tooties on the launcher. Now there are two challenges to the child's imagination. How many Tooties can you stack together on the launcher and how many can you catch once you launch them?

Tooties can also be bounced. The Tootie Bounce should be held parallel to the ground so the Tootie will go straight up. A child can bounce a Tootie to extreme heights when out of doors or in an area with a high roof like a gym. A few practice bounces may be used to gain control before more energetic bounces. Once a child has gained the skill to keep their eyes on the flying Tootie and keep the Tootie flying, a few consecutive high bounces can be exhilarating.

Under the guidance of an optometrist, Tootie tossing and bouncing, can be combined with the use of prisms or other lenses can create additional challenges and learning opportunities.

Tooties are fun! They combine imagination, problem solving, and movement in a series of entertaining and involving activities that challenge the visual process.

The OEP Foundation distributes a great number of publications, tests, and support materials through VisionExtension. However, OEP does not officially endorse any specific product.

The following book, Learning to Learn, discusses activities using the learning development system that has become known as Tooties™. Tooties International is a commercial endeavor. They have graciously allowed the Optometric Extension Program Foundation to reprint this book for our clinical associates.

The activities and concepts illustrated and discussed in this book are based on sound principles of learning and development. The author, as well as Dr. John Hanson, the inventor of Tooties™, understand that while the majority of activities illustrated use Tooties™, the principles involved, as well as many of the activities themselves can be successfully applied without the need to purchase anything from Tooties International (www.tooties.com): or Tooties Europe (www.tootieseurope.com).

Introduction

This manual is meant as a contribution to understanding the power of Tooties and as a guide to give you additional ideas for working with children. If you have Tooties already, you will be able to use them in many different ways, and possibly more effectively than you do already. If you do not have Tooties, you may consider buying them, as Tooties make teaching easier and more fun. If you decide not to buy them, for whatever reason, you can still find very valuable ideas on how to get more out of your teaching skills. While reading this book, think of other tools to use. With ropes and balls, etc., a lot can be achieved as well. Tooties however, make learning how to learn more effective, easy and challenging for children, and even for adults. Teaching can be made easier on the part of the teacher, parent, or therapist, as we learn how to lead children into applying many learning skills simultaneously. Tooties are also a very effective tool to help people who have suffered a loss of various skills and body functions caused by a stroke or an accident, as well as for people who want to improve their overall performance and problem solving skills. In this manual the focus is on teaching children to achieve better in school and to function better during their daily lives.

The word 'child' is used for readability. For the same reason, 'he' is used for all children, whether boy or girl, as this makes expression of ideas easier.

The observations as described in this manual apply to tendencies seen in large groups of children. The situation and approach needed for each individual child can be quite different, and can only be judged after evaluation of current strengths and weaknesses.

It is important that we adapt ourselves to each child's abilities and difficulties. All children benefit tremendously from learning through play and movement with Tooties, or other materials, if the suggested teaching approach is applied.

The order of the exercises in this book is meant as a practical guide to give an overview of the possibilities, and not necessarily intended to suggest a working order. It is advisable to start with the Launcher, as this is the most powerful diagnostic tool to determine what difficulties a child has and how well his self-generated learning abilities have developed. The purpose of this manual is to help you start working with Tooties right away. After careful observation, choose the appropriate exercise to fit each child's current level of skill.

Many years of experience working with Tooties has made it clear that there is a strong relationship between playing, movement and learning. Activities involving movement and play can lead directly to mastering a certain level of self-generated learning abilities when the concepts conveyed in this manual are applied. Activities should have this long-term goal in mind.

Even though the exercises often seem to be very simple, it is recommended that you try them out yourself first. You will find that many of them are not as easy as they appear. After you have experimented yourself, you will have a better feeling for what you are expecting from your pupils. Children who have poor motor control and poor learning skills need to be successful at a task before advancing to the next higher level and more difficult exercises.

It is important to understand that sometimes the beginning, working-level cannot be low enough. Being able to judge this is essential for effective training and good results. It is also important to understand when to continue and allow a child to struggle and learn to really focus, when to persist and not give up right away, and when to stop and change to another exercise.

For teachers and parents it is very important to learn how to be supportive and persistent. Many so-called 'hopeless' children have a lot of potential for improvement as long as supportive circumstances are created for development. When we give up on these children, nobody will ever know how much potential has remained undeveloped, just as many children in school will never know how much they can do when they stop and give up learning.

Human beings as part of nature

The development of living things, whether they are plants, animals or human beings, follows certain patterns according to the laws of nature. One step missed, or partly missed, will influence other steps still to come. A puppy dog locked up in a cage for its first four months, deprived of movement and play with other puppies or humans, will be affected for the rest of his life. Most people will easily understand this. When buying a puppy it is important to check how he has been raised and kept.

For children, similar rules of development apply. We do not put them in cages of course, but we do other things depriving and limiting children of sufficient movement and development, many times unknowingly. Children need time, adequate opportunities, and a supportive environment to be able to develop their full potential. Children, as they are part of nature as well, need to be able to develop accordingly to these laws as much as possible, but many people seem to have forgotten this. For centuries people had to work hard and use their hands and reasoning skills to get that work done. Life was tough, and only simple tools and equipment were available.

Children were able to watch how work was done and learned by participating. Very elementary forces of nature were used like fire, wind and gravity, etc. Toys for children were rare, and if around, they were very simple. The playground was part of nature's garden with many opportunities for learning and understanding the world in which they were living. Helping do the work in and around the house prepared them for life later on. Life was tough and people learned how to survive. They had to be persistent, be concentrated, and put a lot of effort into making a living. People had to use their own knowledge, experience, and creativity to solve problems. This was passed on to their children.

This does not mean that the past should appear more romantic than it really was because life was tough, and other problems existed as well. We only look at the past now as related to the development of many basic learning skills. For centuries and centuries very little changed until the relatively recent introduction of machines, and later computers, into our every day life style.

Today's world

In today's world, many skills people had in the past have disappeared. We have become used to machines and computers taking over. In the beginning, people were probably very happy to be relieved of hard, manual work, but we have become comfortable creatures and many things in our every day lives are now done by computers. We live in an environment where we teach our children how to push the right buttons, and make life as easy as possible. We have vacuum cleaners, washing machines, central heating systems, and parents who work in offices behind computers. Much of the real visible handwork is gone. When we look at this from a child's perspective, we can begin to feel how it is becoming more difficult for them to learn to understand what is really happening in their own and their parent's world. This means that children are frequently deprived of sufficient meaningful experiences and activities, activities that are the foundation for understanding what is later taught in school.

An additional problem is that parents tend to give their children many toys which are designed to entertain rather than to provide useful learning opportunities. We feel life should be easy and this is what we convey to our children as well.

We put our children in front of a television or a computer because that will keep them quiet and it is easy entertainment. This implies that being quiet and not doing anything is better than running around, playing and exploring. We presume children learn from watching television, but in fact, they are only passively observing. No interaction and participation takes place. Parents offer 'exposure' instead of real experience which is not enough for young, developing children. Another important problem is when watching television or playing computer games, children's eyes barely move, as the screen takes over the movement and focussing tasks. Children, however, are still at the stage where important skills need to be developed. When their eyes are not given the opportunities to learn to move and focus properly, they will end up not being able to use their vision as well as they should. This is another big hidden problem as many vision difficulties are not recognized.

When watching television, a child may appear to concentrate but instead, he is pulled towards what is seen on the screen which has nothing to do with active concentration activities. The fact that computer addiction is beginning to become a big problem only adds to the problems children may have already. It provides a strong indication that free will to stop is coming under pressure, and more is happening than just entertainment. Active concentration skills are not being exercised at all as we lead children into being entertained and inactive many hours a day. In addition, playing a video or computer game and watching TV have very little to do with learning to cope with the real world, and it does not teach a child how to learn from and by his own actions and experiences.

We seem to have forgotten that children need to play and move in order to learn and to develop motor skills, vision and reasoning skills. We forget that during the many hours that children watch television or play video games they are not developing these basic learning skills. Planning, structuring, sequencing, concentration, being able to focus and be persistent, being creative, and being able to experiment and learn from it are very important skills to develop.

These skills are needed for learning in school and later for becoming successful. Many children have become very passive and do not know how to get their bodies and brains to work together so they can do what they want to, or do what is expected of them. More and more children grow up with a hidden lack of development, and we cannot imagine the difficulties they begin to run into. Their bodies are not ready to be used as a 'proper tool', nor do they have the right experiences to be ready to learn.

Many children with learning problems have difficulties focusing and concentrating. Their teachers would say that these children are not able to concentrate for more than five minutes. Television screens change images every few seconds, as research has proven that changing the image every few seconds is needed to keep children's attention. This, however, causes children to become used to changes every few seconds. As young children learn by copying you might wonder how they should be able to learn how to concentrate, not to speak of the sleeping difficulties many children have since they have become too restless to relax.

With Tooties, it is possible to teach these children how to extend their attention spans, as we bring them into situations where they learn to concentrate through movement first. When a child has difficulties concentrating while being physically active, imagine how difficult it must be to concentrate just in his mind alone. The mind tends to drift away very easily, and it is very difficult to teach children how to concentrate when they have never (or rarely) had the experience. Many times they do not even know what is meant by 'concentration'. When concentration is exercised while doing a task, a child will be able to feel what it really is. This important learning experience can then be transferred to the learning process later on in school. This is the body teaching the brain how to control thinking and learning abilities.

Another problem is that families today have an average of one, two, or maybe three children. Families with more children are exceptions. We tend to do everything for our children, with the best intentions of giving them everything they need, and frequently we do not have the patience to wait for them to accomplish a task.

We forget to think about what they really need in order to develop basic life skills. We forget to teach and allow children to learn on their own, to think for themselves and solve problems appropriate to their age. Children are able to do so much if only they are allowed to and are given proper guidance. However, many times parents feel they do not have the time or the patience, and not enough learning opportunities are created. Children, however, need guidance and most of them are dependent on what opportunities are offered by their environment. A number of children seem to learn and develop anyway, but many others run into difficulties. We, as adults, are responsible for the world our children live in, and we should provide them with plenty of useful opportunities to develop to the full extent of their capabilities.

Use of toys

Many toys that look appealing to the buyer are designed for temporary use and entertainment. They break easily and when this happens, we just throw them away and buy something new. The value of Tooties is that they are made not only to last over many years, but to keep a child's interest over many years as well. As a child ages, he can use the Tooties in increasingly more creative ways. The inventor, Dr. John Hanson, worked very hard to create something that all ages would enjoy and would not get boring. Although the Tooties materials look very simple, they are very powerful tools. It took years and years of observation and adjusting tiny details to develop them to the perfection they have today. Using them together with the method of indirect teaching, as described in this manual, will provide you with excellent tools to help children discover what they can do, and improve while they are exercising their motor skills.

Tooties can be used as normal toys for children. They are designed to be self-teaching, and children will learn and develop by themselves. Telling them what to do can unintentionally be more harmful to the learning process than it helps. Children who have developed a certain degree of self-generated learning abilities will enjoy playing with them, and they will master many skills all by themselves, including how to learn from failure.

If a child is already afraid of failing or if he does not know how to learn by himself, he will have to be guided through the basic process first, before he will be able to continue alone.

The child as observer rather than participant

All too many of today's children end up being more 'observers' of this world rather than participants and they bring this attitude with them to school. In school, however, children are expected to be active and to be capable of doing many things, as well to exhibit a certain presence of self-generated learning abilities. This means a child has to be able to start learning on his own after the teacher has given instructions. Learning how to read and write is a complicated process by itself, and many basic learning skills are required. The learning process is even more difficult when a child is not ready to learn because of a lack of development. Children's motor and visual skills need to be developed, as well as their thinking skills and self-generated learning abilities. Upon entering school, a child is expected to be able to develop a learning process from within without the constant help of others.

Handling failure

In many situations, failure is avoided rather than treated as an important part of the learning process. Children (and many adults) are afraid of failing.

Opportunities to fail 'safely' are kept away from them and they frequently have not been able to learn how to handle and learn from failure. Failure should be seen as a chance to recognize what does not work, or what is not known, and more importantly, be seen as a chance to try again. Fear of failure handicaps a child's learning process as many children give up before making an effort. The effort needed to master certain skills like sequencing, structuring, planning and persistence, as well as the effort needed to acquire a feeling for quantity, distance, and numbers etc., must be experienced through movement and play first, before a child will be able to properly apply these skills on an abstract level.

Mastering particular skills is much more difficult when failure is seen as a negative experience instead of an essential part of the learning process. Because of this, many children become insecure and develop learning difficulties, as their development slows down tremendously while other children advance to the next levels. Giving up has almost the same effect as when a child is not able to learn at all.

When children grow older, things can get worse as frustration and fear of failure develop further. We need to teach children to be curious and experimental, and to even 'enjoy' failure and to learn from it. Failures should follow the important rules below:

1. It must not hurt anyone.
2. It must not damage anything valuable.
3. It must not take a lot of time, but enough time should be planned in order to provide opportunities to fail and try again.
4. It should be fun.
5. It should insure that success is close, visible and attainable (avoid giving tasks which are too hard to achieve).

Using Tooties is an excellent way to teach children to learn from their own mistakes and to persist until successful. Vision and motor proficiency, as well as thinking and learning skills, are exercised at the same time and become integrated. This is what children need to do in order to become successful.

Parents and teachers presume these basic skills have already developed by the time children have reached a certain age. It is difficult to imagine how an increasing number of children have been unable to master these fundamental skills, and how these children cope in school. What may appear easy to do, can in fact, be very difficult or even impossible for some children. Imagine how a child considered rebellious and hyperactive must feel if we want to teach things not visible or understandable to him! How can we teach reading the clock when we do not realize there are children who do not appear to see the second hand, simply because their vision skills have not properly developed. It also appears to be very difficult for some children to understand what a 'second' really is. This is probably only one of the many little things a child may not be capable of doing, causing part of early school frustration.

Adequate motor skills and perceptual knowledge have frequently not been sufficiently mastered either. Children learn much more from playing and moving than we realize. We as adults tend to look at today's children from our own point of view and from our own experiences. We forget that more and more children do not have the opportunities to develop their basic skills as well as people have been able to in the past.

Value of Tooties

Tooties make it easy to help children catch up in mastering basic skills. The manner of teaching is an essential aid in this process. In the following chapters, it is explained why it is so important to allow children to learn how to learn by themselves, and to teach indirectly. Grasping this concept will help you to help many children even if you do not have Tooties. It is a different way of looking at the learning process and understanding what children really need to become independent from their teacher, parents or therapists. In fact, we do not teach movement but we teach thinking skills. We use movement, however, to help a child learn how to use his brain and body to solve problems he is facing. If he can learn to solve the problem with Tooties, while his body, vision and brain work together, he learns how to learn by himself. We are looking for the learning process behind the movement, as children do learn mainly by movement and by their own experiences. Telling children is not enough. There is a tremendous difference between mere exposure and actual experience.

Tooties as a diagnostic tool

When you take the time and effort to learn the principles behind using Tooties, and begin to observe different children playing with them, you will start to see how children perform without constant help from others, and you will gain even more understanding of how children learn how to learn by themselves. It is very important to observe all children, especially normally developing children in the beginning, even though more and more children nowadays show signs of slow development.

It depends on the standards you have. After observing many children and looking for these particular processes, it becomes obvious how children learn by themselves and how well 'equipped' they are with the basic skills they need. The most valuable aspect to remember when you are working with Tooties is not to explain what to do, not to demonstrate, and not to give direct instructions. When using Tooties as a diagnostic tool, this is most important. We need to understand the learning process to determine if the child is able to generate ideas without the help of others. If a child is unable to catch one Tootie, we can be certain he is likely to have other problems as well. Children in school have to deal with much more complicated issues than this.

It is very important to have children's vision checked by a qualified behavioral optometrist. For addresses please contact us. We can find one in your area. The picture above on the following page is for illustration only and not suitable for testing. Just checking if the child can clearly, see certain sizes of letters from a predetermined distance for a short period of time using the Snellen Chart (20/20 vision), is not enough as many other vision skills need to be developed properly as well. Many vision problems are often not recognized during a standard eye exam since it does not include other ways a child is able to use his vision. Normally, eyes are considered to be working well if there are no physical abnormalities found, and when a child can recognize the symbols or letters. Nevertheless, a child can have many hidden difficulties which are not immediately obvious to parents and teachers. Please read the chapters on vision. There is a list of recommended books and websites on development and vision in the back of this manual as well. As the Launcher is the most powerful tool, a number of skills you want to observe are described in the Launcher chapter. Once you know what the child can and cannot do, you know where to begin helping a child to improve his abilities and skills.

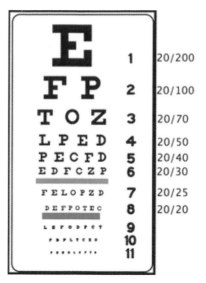

Tooties as a therapeutic tool

We can help children overcome many of their learning difficulties with Tooties when we use them as explained in this manual. Teaching children how to learn, and that learning can be fun, is very rewarding. It can lead children towards an attitude of exploration, and thus, influence their learning skills positively.

Our first goal, in general, is to continually observe a child and see what he is capable of doing. Most importantly, however, we want the child to feel good first. He needs to feel proud of what he can do even when this is much less than the standards we have in mind. Our standards do not have any meaning to the child, and from his perspective, they may be more harmful to him than they are a help. In helping children overcome their difficulties we need to temporarily forget about our standards, go back to the point where the child is successful, and build on this. Many children, especially those who are failing in school have very low self-esteem, as they frequently may feel 'there is something wrong with me'. They are often insecure and afraid of failure. Frequently these children either retreat, become rebellious, or act as clowns in order to attract attention. When we find the level at which the child feels confident, we start to build up from there, and show him that failing is all right as long as he learns something from it.

Many children (and even adults) tend to give up as soon as something gets difficult. This attitude slows down the learning process, adding to the learning difficulties, since they make very little progress while other children continue to learn. The less progress is made, the more frustration builds up within the child and those important people around him. We need to give children the experience that learning can be fun and that 'failure' is a necessary part of the learning process, and can be fun as well. This statement can be found repeatedly in this manual and cannot be emphasized enough.

The material is designed in such a way that it gives a child immediate, understandable visual feedback, which is different from the learning process in school.

In many cases, children do not know if they have done something right or wrong or what is expected from them. That is why many of these children need reassurance all the time and frequently ask: "Did I do this right?" or "Do I have to do it this way?" When the problem is visible for a child he will be more challenged to practice than when the problem is not clear to him at all. Practicing basic learning skills as explained in this manual, in a controlled and safe situation, helps children master them and put them into practice later. With Tooties, failure has no consequences. This is very different from learning situations in school where results are often important. While working with Tooties we can observe many learning skills, detect which part is missing or undeveloped, work on that, and help a child to improve his overall performance and thus become more self-confident.

As a teacher, parent, or therapist using Tooties, we can enjoy the enormous pleasure of complimenting a child and encouraging him to continue. Encouraging a child to continue is, in the beginning, often not that easy and it can be hard work, but once the child gets a taste of success and feels he is improving he will want to continue and learn more. Every child likes to learn if our demands meet his stage of development and he has not been taught to fear failure. Later on in this manual how we can keep children motivated using the right way of complimenting, and how to make the right choice of exercises, is explained. Let the Tooties 'do the negative part' while you do all the nice things like complimenting and encouraging children the right way. This is essential and very important throughout the whole process. Even when a child does something that is way below our expectations, we can still find something to genuinely compliment him on as his performance was the best he could do at that moment.

With Tooties, children immediately see the results of their actions and they have to be allowed to discover and learn what they can do to improve. That is why we do not want to give children direct instructions like: "Throw harder," "Softer," "Higher," "Lower," "Not so sloppy, "Catch," "Stomp harder on the Launcher," "This Tootie is not laying straight," etc. It is very important not to help or demonstrate. Every help or advice is for the child a lost chance to learn.

> ***Our goal is not to teach a child how to catch Tooties, but to go through the learning process behind the activity, which is essential. We want to teach a child to develop his own thinking skills and not be dependent on other people.***

We want to teach him to manage himself and to achieve control from within, without always having to be corrected from an outside person. Learning from his own experience is much more effective than having people telling him what to do. A child has to develop the desire to improve himself because the older he gets, the fewer adults will be around who are willing to help him all the time. Many children with difficulties are being taught to learn and cope with their difficulties instead of being taught to learn how to overcome them. At a certain age, a child is expected to do and judge things himself. But, how will he be able to when he has always been helped by other people?

Our experience shows that it can be very difficult for many people to resist helping a child in the beginning. This teaching technique will seem to take more time, but once the learning process is turned on, a child will start to improve all by himself. Learning is now fun and the results become visible. Once this process is in action a child will continue learning even more because he will be curious about what else he can do and will use all the functions in his brain to experiment and explore.

Another important skill to learn is to be persistent, not give up. Even being physically active is very difficult for many children as they are simply not used to being active for longer periods. This is why it is important to work with a child for a longer period, as much as three hours. Many people think this is impossible and too demanding for a child. But, when you know how to select appropriate exercises and alternatives and change from physically active exercises to the ones where the mind is more involved, it is quite easy to keep a child active and learning. It is important to develop a feeling of when to change activities from the more active exercises to the more relaxing ones, like building roads or towers, while keeping a child's brain working. When children cannot be persistent physically, it is very difficult to develop persistence in their minds alone when trying to master a certain problem.

A child must have experienced skills such as concentration, persistence and structure, etc., through movement and play before he is able to implement these skills at abstract levels, such as math or learning how to read and write.

This manual will give you many ideas for working with children in general, as well as ideas for working with children who have learning difficulties. If you want to learn more about Tootie training, please contact us, and we will help you. We love to come to schools, groups of parents and therapists to demonstrate the power and versatility of Tooties. We can teach you to observe if and how a child is learning and performing. If a teacher or parent is able to better recognize the needs of a child, he will also be better able to help children. Teachers are trained to teach children to read and write but they are not necessarily trained to recognize learning difficulties related to under developed motor and visual skills.

As teachers, therapists, or parents, we can guide children through the learning process using many exercises. We also learn how our own behavior and choices of exercises influence on children's performance. Children react to us and to what we expect from them. If we are able to understand where they are in their learning process and react to that, a child will improve much faster and with much more pleasure.

Teaching children how to time themselves is a very important part of our program. Later in the manual how to use timing and documenting will be explained. It is important to give a child a notebook to write down his scores. It is very rewarding for a child to be able to look back and see how much he has improved. Therefore, it is important to keep the notebook in a safe place, and use it all the time when you are working with the child.

When you work with several children at the same time, it is very important to a child compete with himself instead of with other children. The purpose is to make a child feel he is getting better and not necessarily become better than other children

Competition between children will only make the skilled children feel good about their own abilities. But, the less skilled children will always be the ones to lose, which is very discouraging. Any child can learn to become better. This is what we want to achieve when we time children or when we organize races, etc. A good way is to work is in teams and have each team consist of the same children every day so they can see if they are becoming better as a group. This helps children develop social skills since they learn that they can accomplish more if they support the weaker children to make the group perform better.

When we ask a child to do something again it is very important to make the child aware that starting over is not a punishment, but a new opportunity to learn and to get better!

This gives a different feeling to doing something many times in order to gain proficiency. We want to prevent a child from feeling punished for failing. This is the opposite of the goal we have in mind.

Give a child enough time to go through the process. When working with groups of children in a classroom or outdoors avoid giving turns to other children too quickly. When there are more children than Tootie equipment, it is still best to keep one child on an activity until he improves. Have the other children do something else in the meantime. It is very important to compliment a child frequently during the process, as younger children frequently do not see the achievement behind some of the short-term goals we set.

We wish you a lot of fun using Tooties, and please contact us if you have any questions, suggestions or if you have exercises other people could use. We want to continue collecting exercises and activities and share them with others.

Tootie materials

Former aerospace scientist, Dr. John M. Hanson, who earned his Ph.D. in electronics, invented the Tooties equipment in 1962 to help improve the abilities of his own young children. As the children grew, new types of Tooties and Tooties equipment were developed to address different areas of teaching. When he retired from his successful career he began to focus on developing his teaching program and on perfecting the Tootie equipment.

The goal was to encourage self-teaching and make learning so fun that children would not tire of the games. Gradually, more academics were added to the program in order to combine the use of movement to develop other skills needed for learning in school. John Hanson studied education and psychology in order to better understand why Tooties were so effective in helping children, and even adults. Educators, playground supervisors, parents and optometrists began to discover the immediate benefits and soon Tooties were used in many countries.

Many learning difficulties are a matter of poor development and not necessarily a matter of being inferior or deficient. Exercising body, vision and the mind to work together, as well as developing basic learning skills such as concentration, persistence, structuring and planning, give a child experiences to overcome his difficulties and do much better in school. Tooties are designed to provide exercises for every child at all levels of ability, including handicapped individuals. Begin at each child's current level of functioning and gradually advance to higher levels only when the child is capable. Children love to be challenged as long as they are close to success. Tooties can make teaching children more fun and effective.

John Hanson designed his teaching method to use movement to work on many little things at the same time and to improve such habits like being careless.

Normally developing children who tend to be careless can make many mistakes during the learning process. If a child becomes

Blinking eye

frustrated because of the mistakes he makes and if he also has the tendency to give up easily, his development tends to slow down or even temporarily stop. Telling children to be neat, frequently 'goes in one ear and out the other'. Learning by experience and developing care and persistence is a key to steady improvement. Tooties make the purpose of being neat visible, and encourage children to become neat as they experience the benefits themselves.

In the past there have been attempts to copy the equipment because it seems to be so simple. However, a considerable amount of experimentation and attention was involved to obtain the perfectly-working and powerful tool it is today. This perfection of the Tooties is essential when you work with children as children sense right away when materials do not serve the purpose. In many cases, this is the reason children give up playing with some toys if they break or do not meet their expectations. Many toys are developed to look good, many times for commercial purposes, but they do not necessarily help children develop.

Tootie Launcher

Even though the Launcher (the board) looks very simple, it is a very powerful and versatile tool that has been continually improved during its 40 years of use in practice. For every Tootie Launcher activity it is very important to use a genuine Tootie Launcher even though they appear to be very easy to make. The trajectory of the Tootie is very important and the Launcher is

designed in such a way that it works for all ages. Younger children who do not hit as hard, or do not use their heel where the heel of the footprint is, will not launch a Tootie high enough to be easy to catch.

Another feature of the Launcher is that a Tootie can be launched about 23 feet (7 meters) high quite easily as well. Most children can do this. To catch the Tootie children must learn to step back quite a bit or it will go over their head. Children who do not figure this out themselves are not as well developed as they should be. Encourage them to repeat many times until they do. The Launcher is designed so that it is very sensitive to small differences. It reacts to the user instantly and directly which is very important in a learning process.

Children receive valuable and reliable feedback from their own actions and performance instantly. Consistent and accurate feedback is important when learning a skill.

These attributes make the Launcher a very effective and powerful tool since many motor skills, as well as vision and thinking skills, need to be integrated in order to catch one or more Tooties. Children with poor motor and vision skills will have difficulties launching and catching Tooties, but they will improve their abilities when they continue playing with the Launcher. When the suggested teaching method is applied, the various learning skills will become integrated, providing the best results as well as steady improvement.

Tootie Toss

The Toss (the big net) consists of a net stretched with springs within a frame. The various parts are constructed to provide the best results. The legs are attached to the frame in a way that they can be easily folded. This design makes the Toss very stable as well as easy to carry and put away in a closet or behind a door. Notice that one side is longer than the other. This makes it easy to fit in a car, especially important for travelling teachers, or therapists who need to take the Toss along.

The Toss can be positioned in two different ways just by turning it upside down as two legs are short and two legs are long. When standing on its short legs, the Tooties will bounce back to the thrower softly and gently. This position is suggested when beginning to work with children as young as two years old or younger.

Toddlers love to throw but not catch, and throwing Tooties in the Toss allows them to safely exercise that urge.

When standing on the long legs, the Toss will stand relatively upright and the Tootie will bounce back swiftly, making catching more difficult. Fast reflexes are required. Experiment to see which position is best. It depends on the age and skills of the child, as well as on his position in relation to the Tootie Toss.

Using the Toss will help children to improve their dynamic visual accuracy. If problems in this area are suspected, or show up when using the Toss, it is advisable to start beginners on the Launcher first as visual dynamics are relatively slow with the Launcher. As children become proficient

19–Tootie materials

at catching Tooties with the Launcher, you can decide when to advance to the Toss.

Tootie Bounce

The Bounce (the small net) exists of a small frame, 20 inches square, with a net. One way of using the Bounce is to hold it horizontally and bounce a Tootie vertically. While bouncing the Tootie, the whole body, as well as the eyes, is being exercised. It is a great way to have the child move and exercise motor and visual skills very intensively, especially when used outdoors. The Tootie can be bounced very high. Be careful that the Tootie does not land on a roof or in water as you could lose your valuable Tooties. Our advice is to choose a wide-open space with no electric wires around. If the Bounce is used near water it is recommended to use a Floaty Tootie since it will not sink. If you do want a Tootie to sink, like in a swimming pool, use heavier Classic Tooties. Children, as well as adults, love to dive and try to pick them up. Some children become inventive and blow into the end of the Tootie so that it fills with air and temporarily floats. To maintain the best bouncing quality, the rubber bands should be changed regularly. They age when exposed to sunshine and air as they are made out of natural rubber. If not changed in time, about every three months, or more often depending on use, it is possible the edges of the net will tear. If it does tear, it can be fixed it with some string and knots.

Tooties

Tooties (the bags) come in many different colors, weights, textures, sounds and features. The Classic Tootie, for example, is more 'stable' in comparison to the Floaty Tootie, which is 'livelier', and therefore more difficult to catch.

Of all the various types of Tooties, most people use the same size, usually size 1. Therefore children must touch, squeeze and feel them to tell the differences. That is why Tooties are so useful to teach discrimination and structure.

It is important that children become aware of the just noticeable differences (JNDs). Other sizes of Tooties are available from 0 to 10, but size 1 is still the most popular. For launching Tooties, the differences of the Tooties are not important since all Tooties tend to come up the same way. However, when using the Tooties for throwing and bouncing activities, the differences become very important and can be even critical for best results. Tooties are filled with many special 'bouncing crystals' that give them their different qualities. They are designed very carefully making them unlikely to hurt children even when used carelessly. If you do not wash them or treat them violently, they last at least 10 years. The natural oil of children's hands is absorbed by the cloth and protects it. The more the Tooties are used, the more the bouncing crystals become polished, the better the Tooties feel.

Should it become necessary, most Tooties can be hand-washed with soap and water. Dry with a towel and hang to dry.

Classic Tootie
This is the Tootie (5.25 ounces (151 grams)) used for almost all exercises. It is the easiest to catch, and is the most stable in the assortment. With practice, children 8 years of age or older can throw it under their leg and catch it on top of their head.

The easiest way to catch a Tootie on one's head is by using the Tootie Launcher. More difficult is to throw it under the leg or from the toes and catch. The hardest way is to launch it up with a Tootie Bounce. Sometimes the weight of the Classic is changed by various amounts (up to about plus or minus .35 ounces (10 grams)) so that they are more fun when doing the weighing exercise. If all Tooties would be a perfect 5.25 ounces (151 grams), which can be easily achieved, it would be too easy for children to guess the weight. It takes an extra effort to make them a little different in weight and still not lose their wonderful feeling.

Tweenie Tooties
Tweenies weigh 3.5 ounces (100 grams) and contain a mixture of different crystals. This Tootie is more difficult to catch than the Classic Tootie. The centre of the mass shifts unpredictably to make it jump out of your hands when you least expect it. It feels terrific and can be mixed very well with the crystals found in the Classic Tooties. This one is called a Tweenie Tootie because

in weight it is between a Floaty of 2.5 ounces (70 grams) and a Classic of 5.25 ounces (151 grams). There is a whole family of Tweenies. You can even request custom made Tooties with whatever qualities you like.

Floaty Tooties
Floaties weigh 2.5 ounces (70 grams) and come in various types. They are much lighter and livelier, and they float in water. A Floaty Tootie is the best when you want to use the Bounce outdoors. It can be bounced between 33 and 99 feet (10 or 30 meters), which is an excellent cardio-vascular exercise, leaving almost anyone exhausted in five to 10 minutes. It calms down hyperactive children very quickly while allowing them to get rid of their excess energy, and satisfying their needs for movement.

Squishy Tooties
This new formula of Tootie contents, which was introduced about 1996, has introduced a whole new family of Tooties. Most important is their very interesting feeling and the unusual ways they bounce depending on the formula. Squishy Tooties are especially valuable when training professional baseball and tennis players.

Yaggie and Dreamy Tooties

In general, these weigh about 4.4 ounces (125 grams). They are both filled with the same formula, but the way the ingredients are put together makes them behave differently. In the Yaggie, the heavy Tootie Crystals stay at one end, as they do not like to mix with the lighter crystals. The Dreamy Tootie has a wonderful, soothing feeling. These two products resulted from a fortunate accident during manufacturing when the crystals were 'forced to get along'.

Again, most Tooties are size 1, but there are a variety of other sizes available. The largest size is called the Tootie Baby. It is about the size of a newborn baby and weighs as much as 11 pounds (5 kilograms), but does not hurt when dropped on bare toes. The crystals are designed to shift quickly to distribute the weight evenly. This size can be made in many different weights, from 3 pounds (1.36 kilograms) to 20 pounds (9.07 kilograms) or even more, but 10 pounds (4.53 kilograms)is the most popular.

About 500 Tooties would be the ideal quantity for families with small children or for schools, etc., as children want to have enough available for road building and for making many different kinds of structures. Building things helps children acquire some of the knowledge needed to structure and to plan in advance, as well as to learn elementary physics like balance and gravity. Children learn to become realistic when making plans, and find out what is and what is not possible while exploring and being creative. About three dozen Tooties should be adequate for children over 12 years old, as they usually prefer motor activities over building. Tootie Set 7c includes 32 Tooties of three different types, as well as the other essential Tootie equipment suitable for all ages.

Specialized Tooties

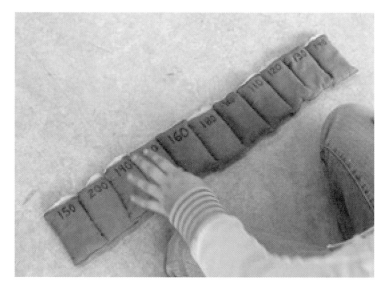

Metric Tooties
A set of 12 Tooties, which all look identical in size and color but are graduated in .35 ounce (10 gram) increments, is available. Place all of them face down and mix them up. Children can take their time putting them in order beginning with the lightest on the left and the heaviest on the right. They may check as many times as they wish, and then turn them over to see how well they did, as the weight is printed on the other side. Most people can do pretty well in discriminating a .35 ounce (10 gram) difference. At first most of the errors will be at the high end where the percentage difference is the least. Always write down the scores so one can see how an individual is improving. This weight set can also be made in .17 ounce (5 gram) increments but discriminating these small differences is very difficult for most people.

Alpha-numeric Tooties
Writing numbers and letters with a marking-pen on individual Tooties can be very useful. The one critical rule that you should follow is that the Tootie label should always be on the left, so that the Tootie closest to the child will be the starting letter. When

teaching children vowels, it is suggested to mark vowels on red Tooties so it is easy to see where the vowels are when spelling words. It can be fun to practice phonics when children are able to catch three or more Tooties successfully. Select the word you want the child to learn, such as 'cat'. Be sure to put the Tootie with a 'C' on the eye (at the end of the board, see diagram on page 17) that blinks when you move position.

When he catches that one he moves the Tootie with 'C' down and adds 'A' on the blinking eye. When he caches these two he adds 'T' on the blinking eye. Every time the child launches, he pronounces the sounds of the letter(s) caught. For example, if the child catches only the 'C' and 'A,' you could help him pronounce 'ca'. If he catches the 'A' and 'T', help him pronounce 'at' and finally all three, 'cat'. Later you can add an 'S' for 'cats'. Think of other possibilities such as 'cattle' 'catches' and 'catching,' etc.

Try other words the same way. The more the child misses the more practice he is getting. You might even consider using more Tooties than he can catch such as the word 'catching' or have him try to catch them in a basket. The last five letters would make a nonsense word 'ching' which could still be pronounced. He can even rearrange the letters he has caught to make other words, so it is important to choose words with more than one vowel. By choosing suitable words the child can improve his vocabulary, spelling and pronunciation. Suitable seven- or eight-letter words can be placed on the Launcher and repeated loading can improve spelling. The more letters are used, the more words a child can make with the letters he caught. Always write each word down on a piece of paper so the child practices his handwriting at the same time. Tooties with numbers can be used the same way for practicing math. When a child catches for example, the numbers 4 and 9 he can lay the corresponding number of Tooties in a matrix, as explained in the math chapter. This will help a child to like math and make math problems visible. Later, he can solve math problems in his mind first, and then lay them in a matrix to check.

Different sized Tooties
Tootie sizes run from 1 to 10. In general they get heavier as the size increases, but there are sets available which go in the reverse direction so that children can learn that objects that are bigger are not always heavier.

It is a very important concept to learn and was prompted by behavioral optometrist Jerry Getman, O.D., Sc.D, who worked closely with John Hanson and Homer H. Hendrickson, O.D., in perfecting the vision benefits of Tooties. The smallest Tooties, size 0, are called Teenie Tooties and can be filled with various substances as well. Teenies were developed for use with the Teenie Tootie Launcher, which is normally used on a table for handicapped children.

Tootie Launcher

The Launcher is the most important and effective piece of all the Tootie equipment. Children love to play with it, trying to see how many Tooties they can catch. When given enough time, any normally developing child will start to improve and learn on his own. After a few hours of practice most children should be able to catch their own age in Tooties or close to it, especially if they have acquired self-generated learning abilities.

The footprint on the Launcher is very important. Observe if the child makes use of this visual clue. Does he hit on the footprint with his whole foot or does he only use his toes, which is less efficient. Some children will even hit above the footprint. Avoid the temptation to instruct children on how to hit the Launcher. Observing their techniques tells us how they learn from experience and can be used for diagnostic purposes described later. It takes a lot of courage on the part of the teacher not to show disappointment but encourage the child to continue and explore. Let a child discover on his own that his technique may not be the most optimal. Some children even launch from the side and still are quite successful, so do not criticize but compliment them on their successes.

The most efficient way of hitting the Launcher is when the heel of one's foot hits the heel of the Launcher footprint just before the rest of the foot. The foot should also remain on the Launcher for a moment to get the most efficient transfer of energy. Hitting with the toes alone can make the Launcher fly up. In this case direct instruction is essential, but do make it as little as possible. Always have the child wear his shoes when working with the Launcher. Socks are slippery and can influence the dynamics of the launches, as well as the results.

How to start

Begin training with one Tootie. If a child wishes to catch more, let him try. Initially keep the process as unstructured as possible. When the child can easily catch two or three Tooties he might be ready for some structure.

Whenever possible try to start with a red Tootie. When the red Tootie can be caught easily, have the child move it down one Tootie width and add a green Tootie on the blinking eye. When a child can catch two Tooties easily, move the others down and add a yellow Tootie on the blinking eye. After being successful with these three Tooties, the next one to be added is a blue one. It is important to always add the new Tootie on the blinking eye. Always put the new Tootie on the far end and keep the red Tootie closest to the child. Let a child continue practicing at his success level before adding another Tootie. Repetition develops confidence and builds stronger foundations. This also contributes to a less stressful experience of this marvelous activity.

Normally all Tooties should touch the board as shown on the picture below. In the beginning you might want to have the child put them any way he wants until he is ready for more structure.

Children with less developed motor skills should be allowed to stack them, as stacked Tooties stay closer to each other when launched. This makes them easier to catch, allowing a child to be more successful. Even tying them together with a rubber band, as well as using a basket as explained later on, can be a valuable help to keep children motivated.

After the blue Tootie feel free to add any different color. If a child has difficulties remembering the sequence, it is important to write it down and place the piece of paper face down. If a child cannot read yet, use colored pencils and mark the sequence with colored dots on the paper. See if a child can remember the sequence from memory and, if necessary, have him turn over the list to verify. It makes a child feel very good when he is right, and the child learns always to check what he is doing. This is very important in the learning process at school. The child is not dependent on what you tell him to be right or wrong, but learns to check if he was right or wrong on his own. This is very important in teaching a child to be responsible for his own learning process and become independent from others.

The color sequence of the first four Tooties should always be red, green, yellow and blue (if available) or any other fixed sequence, as they can give the child a clue if he always misses the lower Tooties, or not. Not having to remember many different sequences is also easier on the teacher.

Sequencing is very important in spelling, reading and math. The Tootie Launcher provides a way to practice this basic skill while having fun. Avoid telling children that the red Tootie will be the lowest when launched and the Tootie on the blinking eye will be the highest. Children who analyze the problem will soon realize they need to catch the lowest Tootie first. After the placement of five Tooties, it is best to allow children to overlap the Tooties a little bit like the tiles on a roof. It is also useful to see how long it takes a child to realize that the eye blinks when the Launcher moves. Many children are not very aware of their surroundings the way they should be.

After some hours of practice normally developing children all over the world can catch about the same number of Tooties as their age. After catching nine Tooties, the task becomes difficult, even for adults. Most people can not catch more than 15 Tooties. For ideas on how to continue and reach this championship level or go beyond it, please check the exercises as described further on.

Tracking and catching difficulties

If a child has difficulties visually tracking a moving Tootie or catching one on his own initiative, he will probably become frustrated and stop playing. These children need guidance to become motivated enough to continue practicing and developing their motor and vision abilities. It is also important to guide children towards developing self-generated learning skills. In this case, use the Tootie Launcher as a diagnostic tool first in order to find out where to begin. You will be able to observe how a child deals with a situation he has never been in before, and if he learns while playing or just does the same thing over again without much success. Observe how he reacts to what happens and how he deals with a problem without anybody telling him what to do. In real life children frequently run into situations where they have to figure out what to do on their own. The older children become, the more often this happens, especially in the learning process at school.

When children are young, people are willing and ready to help all the time, but when children grow older they are expected to handle new and changing situations on their own. When a child is part of a classroom, he will not have a teacher standing next to him all the time telling him what to do. He must learn to solve simple problems by himself in order to make progress without constant help. If a young child has not had sufficient opportunities to learn to use his mind and body adequately, dealing with more complicated problems and solving them will be more difficult as he becomes older. Children need to be taught to learn how to learn on their own in order to be more successful and happy in school and in real life situations.

Consulting a behavioral optometrist in your area is very important in cases of suspected vision problems. He or she is an expert who can give you advice for specific problems. Vision problems are almost never isolated problems. Frequently, difficulties appear because of a general lack of developmental opportunities. Consultations are important to make sure no real physical defects in the eye itself are the cause. Problems due to a lack of development can be trained and overcome in most cases. Tooties can be very helpful in visual training exercises, and many behavioral optometrists around the world use Tooties for vision training. Please check the chapter on vision for more information. Having 20/20 vision is not enough.

Diversionary tactics

If a child seems to be getting frustrated it is important to temporarily change activities to something else before going back to the original exercise. You can switch to simple exercises like jumping with a Tootie under the chin or building towers. These exercises are described in the chapter about the use of Tooties only.

Use as a diagnostic tool

Give a child a Launcher and one Tootie. Be sure the Tootie has a color that is easy to see and different from the color of the background. Red is usually the best color for many reasons. Do not give instructions on how to launch and do not say that he is supposed to catch it, but observe the child carefully. It is ESSENTIAL neither to tell the child what to do, nor to demonstrate or give direct guidance. Just give him the simple instruction: "Put the Tootie on the Launcher, then stomp on the other end and see what happens." If the child should ask you what he should do, just smile and say that he should see for himself what is going to happen.

Many children are used to being given direct instructions and helped by an adult right away. Therefore they want to know exactly what is going to happen, before they even try something on their own. This can become a serious problem in school as a child waits to be told what to do and exactly how to do it. This slows down the learning process very quickly as teachers are not constantly available to help each individual child right away.

Many times a child becomes insecure and is afraid of doing something wrong. Other times a child has difficulties solving a problem on his own. This makes a child completely dependent on other people to tell him what to do next.

Observations

Tracking: As mentioned before, it is very important to see if a child is able to visually track the Tootie. If he has difficulties, do not tell him to watch the Tootie, but encourage him to keep on launching. Normally a child's tracking abilities will improve. It is very important that his desire to track comes from within and not from an adult who can obviously see that the child is not visually tracking. Children should be able to track properly

right away or at least after a few tries. Sometimes a child follows the Tootie as it flies up but loses it when it moves above eye level. Many children seem to have an imaginary visual stop at eye level and cannot see above that. It is important to open this part of the visual field. The picture at left clearly shows the child has no idea of where the red Tootie is, nor does he make any attempt to catch it.

You will see some children launching a Tootie, standing still, staring straight forward and waiting until they hear the Tootie drop on the floor. They will look for the Tootie and then continue. Be sure to compliment the child, and wait for the moment they put some more effort in trying to track or to catch. Complimenting children on every tiny improvement keeps them motivated to continue. Poor tracking abilities are often signs of poorly developed visual motor skills. These motor skills, however, are very important for learning to read and write. Please check the chapter on vision for more details.

If a child continues to have difficulties tracking and it becomes obvious that improvement is not likely to happen, use a basket as an aid to catch the Tootie or use the Tootie bounce with a balloon. This will keep the child motivated and will give relief when success is still far away. Please check the exercises described further on. Be sure to allow enough time to practice before changing activities.

Catching: Does the child make any attempt to catch or does he not even move his hands as if wanting to catch? Normally children should try to catch, as they will predict that while stomping at one end, the Tootie will come up. Trying to catch is a normal reaction. It is possible that some children do not make an attempt to catch because they have not been told to do so. Such children may be so conditioned to help from adults or older siblings that they do not think for themselves. One of the goals of this program is to reverse that negative conditioning as soon as possible.

If the child does stretch his arms, does he make any effort to catch or is he just waiting for the Tootie to fall into his arms? This passive attitude yields few results in learning. When this happens, encourage the child to continue trying and look for progress to compliment him.

If the child continues having difficulties catching try giving him a basket or a plate and see what happens. With this aid he will have the success he needs to keep motivated and continue practicing. He still continues to exercise control of his legs, feet, arms and eyes, while practicing how to stomp and keep the basket straight. For some children this may be quite difficult in the beginning. If you need to use a basket or a plate, consider using more than one Tootie on the Launcher to improve the likelihood of one landing in the basket.

Motor skills: Observe the child when he tries to catch. Does he know where to intercept or does he always just miss the Tootie? This may indicate how well the eyes are working together. The child may have difficulty predicting where the Tootie is in space.

If the child catches the Tootie, does he appear to be self confident or does he catch in an insecure or inefficient way? This shows much about how a child is actually performing in other learning situations where his problems are more difficult to observe. If you have seen a sufficient number of children with these problems using Tooties you will recognize visual and motor difficulties quickly even without Tooties. You will start recognizing them when you observe children move and respond.

A lack of proper motor skills often causes children to be insecure. They are simply not skilled enough to know how to put their body into action properly in order to accomplish what they want. A child having difficulties in these areas needs a lot of practice. He needs to learn to move and use his body efficiently as this will help him to perform much better and gain self confidence. In addition, he will be able to start doing more things simultaneously which is also needed when learning to read and write. A child's body is most effective when it is controlled on a subconscious level. His energy can then be used to focus on other things like reading, comprehension and writing. Most schools expect that basic learning skills are already present. If not, there is generally little or no opportunity for children to catch up with these basic skills without falling behind.

Learning: Observe if a child improves with each launch or if he keeps doing the same thing over and over again. Quite a number of children do not seem to learn from their mistakes, or from what is happening in a particular situation. They seem unable to change their strategy after they see what they do does not work.

Does a child learn from his own actions? Does he know, for example, when the Tootie does not go high enough that he needs to stomp harder? How long does it take him to figure out things like this by himself? In other words, is there an independent learning process going without others telling him what to do? This is what we are looking for, as the child with undeveloped motor and visual skills often has not been able to master these learning skills either. These skills, however, are essential for the learning process in school.

In the complicated learning process in school this behavior is more likely hidden and frequently overseen. But with Tooties this attitude is easy to observe. When there is no learning or very little learning going on with Tooties, the same is very likely happening in other situations as well. When using Tooties the learning situation is more visible to a child and when he learns to improve his learning skills with Tooties he then can transfer these skills to other learning situations later.

Hand and foot preferences: You can see right away which hand and foot a child prefers to use. When he gets better at catching, ask him if he can catch with one hand. Next, observe what happens when you ask him to catch with the other hand. Does he also change his foot? Some children tend to change from using their right foot and right hand, to their left foot and left hand. In other words, you can observe if a child is able to cross his middle line which is very important.

Controlling force: Is a child able to use the right amount of force while stomping on the Launcher? Some children stomp too softly or too hard, which is normal in the beginning. Observe how many attempts it takes to use the correct amount of force. Be aware of body language and avoid showing any disappointment.

When a child stomps too hard and the Tootie hits the ceiling, let him know that what he did was interesting. Then ask him to launch in such a way that the Tootie does not hit the ceiling. Let him repeat several times to see if he adjusts his force. Another way is to suggest launching the Tootie in such a manner that it does not hit the ceiling but just barely touches it. In this way he has to be able to control his force from within, and he has to use his thinking skills to figure out what to do rather than you telling him to hit not quite as hard. It is very important to give children positive feedback instead of forbidding them to do something, like making the Tootie hit the ceiling. When a child figures out how to control his force he has made a step in learning to learn on his own, and he is not just doing as he has been told. Many children have difficulties putting the right amount of force into doing something causing a lot of problems in many areas, including social skills. Control from within is a step towards real improvement and indirect teaching is the secret. It does take more time, but it is worth it.

Handling failure: Many children do not know how to handle failure. They become frustrated and give up without knowing how much they would be able to do if only they were persistent and did not give up. Our attitude can have a considerable effect on how children respond and behave. Children sense when we are not happy and feel our disappointment with what they do.

Failing becomes a negative experience. If we show a child respect for what he does and ask him to try it again, it is more likely that he will be willing to continue. Encouraging a child to repeat a task (using direct instruction only when necessary) is very important. Give direct instructions only in situations where a child might harm himself or things in the room.

The Tooties System is designed to make a child successful, become proficient and then advance to the next level. This will motivate him to continue and give him the experience of getting better as long as he does not give up. Gradually he will improve and, step-by-step, more difficult tasks can be added. The child will see the progress he is making, which is very rewarding and encouraging. Finally, he will be motivated to continue even when he really has to struggle hard. It is VERY IMPORTANT to allow a child to struggle 'within reason'. At this time a child begins to use his observation and thinking skills to solve a problem, and this is what we are looking for. When you see a child become frustrated you will have to decide if it would be important for him to continue anyway, or if it is time to deviate and come back to this particular exercise after some time off. You will have to develop a sense for this. It is very important to know when to stop, and when to continue. Each child needs a different approach.

The goal of the Tooties System is not just to teach catching, even though this is a very valuable and important skill, but to teach a child how to learn on his own. If a child is able to learn through motor activities, he will be able to apply these learning skills in other situations as well as to solve abstract problems in school. Tooties are powerful if we teach using an indirect method instead of a direct method. Failure is often not seen as part of the learning process and therefore can be frightening. Using the Launcher as a diagnostic tool permits you to observe a child in situations he has never been in before and to see how he handles failure. Writing down the results of his attempts, as described later on, will help him see he is improving, and give him the experience that failing is part of the learning process. When he sees his improvements in writing he will be able to look back and see how much he has accomplished already. This is a very valuable experience to help the child overcome fear of failure.

Persistence: Observe if a child is willing to work hard or if he frequently complains. In other words, does a child show some persistence or does he readily give up. Many children tend to give up as soon as they have to perform on heir own. Some children do work *until you turn your back to them* and then they stop right away. They need the attention of a complimenting adult in order to be active or keep motivated. Many of these children are not used to problem solving and tend to 'sit around' with few opportunities to learn. It is very important for children to discover that they can achieve much more than they think they can and that to become successful, effort, practice and repetition are needed.

Problems naturally occur in life. In order to master them children have to learn to be persistent when necessary and not to give up. If a child gives up too early he will never know what he is capable of doing. This is very important to learn since many children give up before they even try. Learning and problem-solving in school can be a difficult process for some children. When difficulties are always kept away from a child, he learns to avoid exerting an effort because he has always been given the message that exerting an effort is a waste of time. Some children may never have learned HOW to put an effort into achieving something. They have been assisted so much that they have become lazy in this respect. This attitude is one of the ingredients for developing learning difficulties in school. There is no teacher who can continually sit next to an individual child to tell him what to do.

For observing adults, it can be very painful to see a child struggle even when the situation is safe. Being able and willing to struggle, however, is very important for the learning process. As long as we keep this in mind observing this process should not be so hard or painful.

It is very interesting, indeed, to observe how well the self-generated learning ability of a child begins to develop. Being able and willing to struggle, learn from failure and not give up are the ingredients for success in many situations. Ask successful business people and they will agree with this. *Therefore, helping children too much, preventing them from learning to learn on their own, can harm them.* We need to assist children to confront frustration and to become independent learners even if it may make us feel good to help a child feel happy by quickly stepping in to help. Quickly helping is a short-term solution. We need to take the time, have the patience and keep the long-term benefits in mind!! *As soon as we are able to really grasp this teaching concept, we will understand that it not only applies to all teaching activities with Tooties, but applies to many other teaching situations as well.* It is very important that no matter what the child does, we find something positive to say about it. Stimulate him to continue by saying: "Oh, that was great how you stomped on the Launcher, do it again." Just by keeping the child active and thinking we will help him to learn how to learn on his own.

Some children do not know how to co-ordinate their hands at the midline to catch two or three Tooties, or cannot imagine how one can catch three Tooties using only two hands. Let them figure out how to solve this problem. They have to learn to look at a problem from various points of view. When children have been encouraged to work hard and not to give up, they eventually will discover that they are capable of catching even seven or eight Tooties without any problem. Children learn a very valuable lesson from their own meaningful experiences. They also learn that they can do much more than they thought they could. This is much more effective than other people just telling a child what to do. On future learning occasions, a child will be more willing to put an effort into trying to master a task as he now has experienced that hard work does pay off and will be rewarding. If a child gives up without even trying, he is almost as handicapped as if he were not able to do it at all. Children with an attitude like this will never discover what they are capable of doing, and this is a waste of so much potential. They will end up being unhappy about themselves and have very little self-esteem.

Once they have had a taste of success, it is much easier to motivate them to continue and try other alternatives. This experience is also valuable later in life.

Use of other senses: If a child does not catch the Tootie and it drops on the floor, observe his response. Does he immediately look in the right direction, or does he appear to be unaware of where the Tootie went? In other words, is he using other senses than vision? When a child is not able to track the Tooties with his eyes, does he hear where the Tootie dropped on the floor? Some children search all over for the Tootie as they have no idea where it went. When a child goes directly to where the Tootie dropped, you know that he is able to locate where the Tootie went. Be sure to compliment him on that and encourage him to continue. Many children with difficulties have no idea of where the Tootie fell, especially if it went over their head. Learn to avoid making negative comments about a child's current level of skill. After a child has found the Tootie just encourage him to launch again.

Fear: Is a child afraid of the Tootie? This often is a sign that a child does not see where the Tootie goes. Children with poor tracking abilities have difficulties seeing moving objects. This can make them feel very insecure and unsafe. This kind of fear is very likely to show up in other situations also. Being among other children who are moving around fast can be difficult for them if they cannot easily see or locate where children go or where they come from. Playgrounds and physical education lessons can become places where a child does not feel at ease, and this will prevent him from participation.

Following instructions: When you give a child a simple instruction like, "Put a Tootie on the Launcher and stomp on the other end," is he able to follow the instruction or do you have to repeat or encourage him to start? This gives an impression of how a child understands and follows instructions in general. Some children are used to people telling them the same thing several times. They appear to have stopped paying attention to what was said the first time and seem to start listening only after the instruction has been repeated several times. It is important to teach children to listen the first time and not repeat if they do not listen. It is hard, sometimes, to let children suffer a little but it makes them aware of what happens when they do not pay attention to what is said.

Slow versus active: Observe if a child is responding slowly or actively. Some children respond so slowly that they have problems keeping up with the learning process in school. Using Tooties and having them time themselves, as described later, will encourage them to become more actively involved in what they are doing. The scores will prove they do much better when they become more actively involved. Some children never seem to have had this experience before and find it difficult to take an active part in learning simply because they do not know how. Once children have had the experience they will be able to do it again. And as we all know, 'practice makes perfect'.

Communication and behavior: It is important to become more aware of our facial gestures and the impact they can have. Children are very sensitive and should get the message that we are honest about our comments. They can tell right away if we are just pretending. We have to realize that at any one moment a child is doing the best he can. Even when a child behaves in an uncontrolled way, he shows right away what his problems are. As parents, teachers and therapists, we should guide children by using indirect teaching as this helps develop self-control and critical thinking skills. These skills can be applied to other situations in the future and we need to give children experience in handling them. Our job, as a teacher or parent, is to encourage and motivate children so they want to investigate by themselves.

At first you may need to compliment them a lot for whatever they do but gradually inner motivation develops. That is what we are looking for. When a child learns to use his body, mind and thinking skills as 'proper tools', and to persist and not give up when things appear to be difficult, he will be able to solve many problems later in life as well.

Once you gain experience observing children in this way and you know what to look for, you will start to recognize many different problems that prevent children from learning efficiently. Studying the self-generated learning process carefully will help you to observe how complicated learning really is and how many skills are actually needed, and still need to be developed. The problem is that these skills are expected to be present and the majority of them functioning when a child begins to learn to read and write. Unfortunately all too many of today's children have not been able to master them. It is very sad that the lack of basic skills caused by the environment prevents children from performing on a so-called normal level. In many cases, children are labeled 'learning disabled', which frequently means that there is a problem which cannot be 'cured'. With Tooties, however, we can still give children plenty of opportunities to develop and learn how to learn on their own.

The most beautiful feature of the Launcher is that it can be easily used to observe children's behavior, reactions and problems as well as a fun and interesting training tool to help children produce immediate and steady improvement. Therefore, it is important to keep notes when a child begins any work on the Launcher. Later, it is difficult to remember what the child did and exactly what the problems were.

Use as a therapeutic and working tool

Once we know what the child can and cannot do, we grasp onto this and use it as a starting point for improvement. Sometimes we have to go way back from what we think a child of a certain age should be able to do. Exercising very basic skills is important as these are very essential for a child to rely on. Our goal is to find something a child is capable of doing and have him practice until he can do this really well. When that is easy, then it is time to add the next new small step. Be careful not to make the next step too difficult. The goal should always be within reach. It is most important to give the child the opportunity to be close to success otherwise it is very likely he will lose his motivation to continue.

In the beginning practicing with just one Tootie can be enough for motorically less developed children. If catching is too difficult, allow him to practice tracking as an isolated skill first. Tracking is an important skill and exercise in itself, especially if a child is not ready to combine various motor and learning skills to do more things at the same time. Use the Tootie Bounce with a large round balloon, as described in this manual, if children continue to have tracking difficulties. As they get better use smaller balloons by filling them with less air. Giving a child a basket to catch the Tooties with can be a very good help as well. In time, children eventually begin attempts to catch with their hands on their own initiative, and that is what we are looking for.

Patience, giving children time to experiment, and praise are important. Acknowledge achievements and encourage children to continue even when they do things other than what we have in mind. As long as a thinking process can be observed, and a child is achieving even the tiniest results, it is important to stimulate him to continue and feel genuinely happy with his progress. Remember, only set limits if safety is a factor.

The exercises to follow can be used to gradually advance to more complex levels of challenge. None of the exercises has fixed rules, so feel free to use many other ways to keep children going and motivated to learn. Avoid frustrating children by setting goals that are too high. Teachers need to be aware of this. They need to master the ability to examine a task and judge on the spot what exercise would be the most suitable for a child to do, or what would be too difficult or challenging at the moment. We do not want to frustrate a child even though sometimes this cannot be completely avoided. Learning can be fun and motivating but always remember that success has to be close, otherwise a child will lose motivation very quickly. We all grow while confronting a reasonable, just-obtainable challenge, but lose motivation when goals are too high. Children should not be blamed for what they cannot do. It is our job to evaluate what they need to make it work. A slight change of activity can be the key to success and motivate a child to continue. When you see a child is ready to start catching more Tooties, a second Tootie can be added. Make sure the last task was easy and a child feels confident before proceeding to the next level. Remember, always try to start with a red Tootie, and follow with a green, yellow and blue one, as described earlier.

Sequencing

Remembering a sequence is not only a very important learning skill, but a very important and effective visual exercise as well. Children have to be able to quickly recognize when something is wrong in a sequence. With Tooties, the visual quality of the game makes it easy to understand and proves to a child if his memory is right or wrong. Writing down the sequence or making a sequence of colored dots in a child's notebook allows him to check his results and become independent of another person's judgment.

Or, put the same sequence of Tooties in a row next to the Launcher, allowing him to check. When he gradually improves his sequential memory, the row can be moved further away, and later covered by a towel or any other piece of cloth. The child has to put the Tooties on the Launcher, think if the sequence is right, check and adjust the sequence, and say out loud if he was right or wrong. By gradually encouraging the child to remember first before peeking under the towel, the child will gain confidence when he checks himself and discovers he is right. If he is not right, he can still rely on the sequence under the towel. In this way, we do not have to correct a child all the time. Many children who have problems are continually corrected without being aware of what people really expect from them. In this way Tooties help a child correct his errors, and become aware of them. A positive attitude makes learning more fun, interesting and exciting, as there is no negative path to failure.

Reading and writing is difficult for a child if he does not adequately understand and cannot apply correct sound/letter associations. If a child has difficulties visualizing and sequencing letters as well, it adds more to the confusion. Memorizing Tootie sequences can help practice this skill in another form. If a child learns to keep the right sequence of Tooties, he will be more likely to recognize sequences in other situations as well. Focusing on sequences can help eliminate one problem in this learning process, which will make it easier for a child to focus on recognizing the letters of the alphabet later.

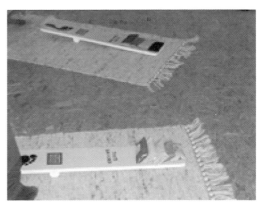

When a child catches up to five Tooties tell him (one of the few times we use direct teaching) he is allowed to overlap them, like the tiles on a roof, as shown in the example at right. Tooties should not be stacked unless a child is operating at a very low level.

In that case, you might use a rubber band to hold the Tooties together. A child still gets to practice launching and tracking more Tooties. Stacking is very useful for special needs children as the Tooties stay closer to each other in the air when stacked and, therefore, easier to catch. Using a strong rubber band to hold the Tooties together can be very useful to keep the child motivated as he still sees progress when adding more Tooties.

When the child starts catching more than four Tooties he can overlap them as indicated before. A child might also discover that he can load the Launcher as shown in the picture at left which is also a good way because the Tooties will stay close to each other after launching. But avoid telling a child this. He needs to discover this himself.

When you notice a child putting the wrong sequence on the Launcher, you should not tell him but say something like, "Uh-oh," and use your voice to make him aware that he needs to pay attention to something. He should get the message that he has to check himself and find out what was wrong. Again, we use direct teaching as little as possible!

There might be situations in which a child is not advanced enough to launch and catch because of weak or lacking motor and visual skills. Many times remembering a sequence puts too much pressure on him so avoid advancing to this level too quickly. In this case, you might consider allowing him to omit the sequencing but do not forget to fold this in as soon as you feel he is ready for it. Learning to remember the correct sequence is very important in many learning situations.

Math, letters in a row forming a word, words in a row forming a sentence, and remembering the right telephone number all have to do with sequencing. Many children who have dyslexia show a lack of sequencing skills. Children benefit overall from direct experience, from actually feeling what comes first, what is next, and so on. This motor experience paired with a positive attitude helps develop an internal sense and internal reference which will support a child throughout his learning experiences. It is much more meaningful than solely relying on other people to keep telling a child what he should do next.

For a teacher, it is important to see if a child misses the same Tootie over and over again. If a child always misses the red one, you know he does not put his hands low enough or launch hard enough. Avoid telling him, as it is important for a child to figure this out all by himself. When he does the same thing wrong all the time he should start wondering why.

Notice that while catching, children rely on the use of their proprioceptive sense to know where their body and hands are. The picture on the right shows how one has to look at all the Tooties when catching, and not just look at the hands. It is important to feel and to learn to know exactly where your hands are in space in order to be able to catch that many Tooties.

Having a child time himself with a stopwatch can be a great challenge and it will encourage him to continue, as he will have a new chance to get better all the time.

It is fun to write scores down and have a child verbalize if he did better than the last time. Children are very proud when they see they are improving It motivates them to learn and they enjoy making progress. This is what we are looking for and it is an important goal. Ask a child, for example, to see how many times he can launch one Tootie in two or three minutes. Whether he catches it is not important at this stage but a child should discover after some time that he can make more launches in two minutes if he catches the Tootie because he can put it back on the Launcher again. After he becomes better at catching, have him time how many times he can catch a Tootie in two or more minutes, and this becomes another new challenge.

As a child continually improves, he can time himself with a stopwatch and see how long it takes to catch, for example five Tooties at the same time. Start with one, and remember to keep the right sequence. Write down the times so he will see for himself that he is making progress. A stopwatch with a wristband is the best. This will make a child perform more efficiently, give him the motivation to do the same thing over and over again, and practice a lot as well which is what he really needs. Children need to learn how to perform physically on an automatic and effortless level without having to pay additional attention to the actual act of carrying out a physical activity. Children who need to put too much effort into controlling their body (and vision) while writing or reading have less energy left for the important task of understanding. The 'simple' doing of more than two things at once becomes difficult. A form is included at the end of this manual to write down the sequences, the time needed and the number of attempts.

Exercises with one Tootie

As mentioned before, it is important to encourage children who have difficulties to develop their abilities to the point that they can easily catch one Tootie. Up to that point in time we should be happy with any improvement, even the tiniest possible. Even if a child is still unable to catch, he is at least moving, exercising his legs, his vision and his hearing.

Learning to observe and acknowledge children's abilities during the learning process is fascinating. Teaching this way takes a lot of patience but the results are very rewarding. Allow yourself the time to go back as far as possible, until you find something the child can do, even though you know he should be performing far beyond this level. Start gradually building upon that, and the child will gradually learn to overcome his fears and difficulties. It is very important to allow children to become good at something first before advancing to the next level because they are frequently overloaded. All children love the feeling of being capable of doing something correctly. We want to connect to this and build self esteem. It is very important to compliment children on the things they do right like starting to track the Tootie with their eyes. If a child was earlier unable to do this, this is a big achievement. Even pointing at a Tootie moving in the air can be a valuable exercise to keep a child going and gradually gain improvement. When a Tootie hits a child's hand by accident, it is important to compliment him, as this is when he gets the message indirectly that trying to catch might be a possibility. Say something like, "Wow, you touched it." When a child comes to the point of starting to catch, or if he has done this from the beginning, you can start building up the exercise. But remember, it is important to allow a child to become really good and efficient at something before you go to the next step. Of course, you can go to another exercise like sitting down and standing up with a Tootie on the head or building towers when you see a child is getting too much of a particular exercise and needs some variation. In this way, you allow a child a bit of relief for a short time. You still keep him concentrated but in another way. It is very important to go back to the first exercise after a while so he will learn persistence. Many times improvement is seen after going back and this will make the child feel good. At all levels of school there is a tendency to push students to the next level before they have established a firm foundation at lower levels. This is why with Tooties (and with school skills like math) you allow a child to get really good before tackling the next level. Allow them to jump ahead if they wish, and go back down in order to get more practice if they feel it is necessary.

Begin by asking a child to start counting how many times he can catch one single Tootie. If the Tootie drops on the floor, he continues counting the next catch. Catch with two hands first, as this is easier than catching with one hand.

Later, you can ask a child to start counting how many times he can catch a Tootie without dropping it on the floor. If the Tootie drops, he has to start counting from the beginning. When the child complains that he is being punished for missing, it is very important to tell him that it is not a punishment but a new opportunity to get better. In the mean time, we always use a positive approach and constantly monitor our tone of voice and body language. Counting catches is a great exercise for all children, as many of those with motor and visual problems are more likely to develop learning difficulties. Counting over and over again has two important values. First, the child sees that he is getting better when he starts catching the Tootie more times than he drops it. It is very important that a child experiences his own success and sees for himself that he is improving. The second benefit is that practice counting will improve a child's math. Many children who have difficulties with math have no idea about numbers and the quantities they represent. Counting over and over again will give the child the very important feeling of the meaning of numbers. As motor skills develop, a child gets to count further. When numbers become meaningful to a child it will be easier for him to start adding and subtracting. Compliment the child when he tries to catch with one hand by himself, and encourage him to continue doing this. Counting catches will continue to be important as a child benefits from many opportunities to count over and over again. We want children to learn to count automatically without having to think about it. When catching with the preferred hand is easy, you might suggest a switch to catching with the other hand. Catching with the opposite hand to the leg that is stomping will teach the child to cross his midline. Also try to the other way around. Timing with a stopwatch as indicated above and creating more exercises yourself will make the whole process fun for both you and the child.

Using a basket

Using a basket is invaluable when working with motorically less developed children. The surface of the basket is naturally bigger than the hands alone, and therefore, it is more likely that a Tootie will drop in. In the beginning you might want to use more Tooties to make it more likely that at least one will fall in accidentally.

Using the basket relieves the hands from catching and simplifies the activity for a less coordinated child. Now he can pay more attention to using his vision and legs. When a child is ready to count, have him count out loud the number of Tooties he catches. The more Tooties he catches, the heavier the basket becomes. This aids in strengthening the upper body muscles.

Children are very pleased when they see the number of Tooties in the basket, as this shows their achievement. Give a child the opportunity to do this as many times as necessary before advancing to the next level. It is important for us to develop patience and not expect too much too soon. When a child improves, ask him to start with one Tootie and count how many times he can catch the Tootie in the basket. When he gets better you can have him start counting the ones he can catch without missing and go up as far as even one hundred. As mentioned before, this is a great exercise for the less skillful child. Other children, however, love to do this exercise as well.

Catching a Tootie in a basket on one's head

This is a great exercise to switch to when you see a child getting bored or frustrated with a particular exercise. Children often get bored or frustrated when they have not been successful for some time. When you see that success is still far from reach, you might want to switch to another exercise for a while. Some children, however, can get bored very quickly and give up when they think something is too difficult. In this case, we do not want to allow the child to stop but exercise persistence.

Deviating to another exercise for a while can add diversity, but always return to the same exercise. This can be very important and powerful in these cases.

Have a child catch one Tootie at first, empty the basket and catch one again. Later he might try how many single Tooties he can catch and still keep the basket on his head. The basket gradually gains in weight and supports the development of the head and neck muscles. If a child is ready, he might even try to catch more Tooties launched at the same time. Changing to this exercise will also give some relief, as most children like this challenge when they are past the lowest level of performance. The secret is to keep them going even when this is difficult to do.

Changing from one exercise to another and then returning to the original exercise is a good way to keep children moving and keep their minds working. It is important to teach a child not to give up but go back to the problem and try again. Quite often you will see a child become successful even when earlier no progress could be seen.

The Launcher as a balance board

Have a child on the Launcher using it as a balance board. When he is ready, put one Tootie on his head and have him try to keep it there. When he gets better, you can have him put the Tootie on his head himself. If a child has difficulties with his feet positioned as shown in the picture on the left, then have him try with each foot the same distance from the pivot point. As he gets better, he might be able to have one foot on the footprint and other on the blinking eye, which is more difficult. Later, you can build small towers on his head, starting with two or three Tooties laid criss-cross. See how many he can keep on his head without losing his balance. Of course, the child can try to make a tower on his head himself. To make it even more difficult, experiment building small towers on a child's shoulders as well. This is a great way to exercise balance and body awareness. At first, the Tooties should be stacked in a criss-cross manner, as this is easier.

Launching back to front

Have a child put one Tootie on the Launcher and launch with his back to the Launcher. Since he cannot see the Tootie, he has to learn to estimate how hard he has to stomp so that the Tootie goes high enough over his head in order to be able to catch it. He will also have to predict where the Tootie will be without seeing it flying up.

Now a child has to use his 'inner vision', and be fast in tracking in order to catch the Tootie before it touches the floor. This is difficult for many children, and in the beginning they tend to turn around to catch, which of course is allowed until they are ready to do it without turning around. Some children grasp the concept immediately and can visualize what happens behind their back. Other children really need their eyes in the beginning because they just do not know how the Tootie goes over their head. Gradually they will get better and learn how to do it without turning around.

From Launcher to Bounce

In order to keep the exercises exciting you may create many different kinds of combinations using the Tooties equipment. Children love to experiment and they should be allowed to do so. In that way we are able to learn from them as well, and we may see a few new and valuable ways of using Tooties. In the exercise shown in the picture on the right, the child launches the Tootie with his foot, and then needs to 'give a little' with his knees when the Tootie lands on the net or it will bounce off. The child can continue bouncing the Tootie with the bounce as well, until it drops. Then the child can launch the Tootie again.

Launching a Tootie and catching it on one's head

This is a very good exercise to encourage persistence. In the beginning, this may seem impossible to do, and it does require quite a bit of body control to succeed. Have the child practice touching the Tootie with his head first. When 'only' touching becomes easy, the child can begin to practice catching the Tootie on top of his head.

The secret is to launch the Tootie with the right amount of force so it reaches the 'dead point' at the height of the head. Now the child has only to put his head underneath the Tootie. Be sure not to tell this to the child. Let him discover. Catching a Tootie on one's head using the Launcher is easier than throwing a Tootie under the leg and catching it on one's head, as explained in the chapter on Tooties only.

Use a Regular Tootie. This is the most stable one and therefore the easiest for this exercise. Almost any normal child of 8 years old can do this within several hours of practice. Gradually the Tootie will linger longer and longer on a child's head. This is highly motivating, as the child can feel he is close to success. When it does stay on top of the head the child has a marvelous feeling of achievement and is willing to try it again. If a child or adult is having trouble, you may notice a number of errors, such as launching too high so the Tootie picks up too much speed coming down and bouncing off the head. Avoid telling a child but take a break and do the following preliminary exercise that will make it easier. Have a child stand with a Classic Tootie on his head and do a small jump so that the Tootie leaves his head about an inch and returns back on his head. Practice until he can do it 10 or more times without missing. Be sure to have children stop and briefly pause after each jump.

They are not allowed to adjust the Tootie with their hands but the delay gives them time to think of how to jump in order to get the Tootie back to the center of their head if it lands to one side. Technically, catching a Tootie on the head is quite a difficult task. It requires an individual to know where his head is in space and where the Tootie will be at the moment it is supposed to land on his head. Each time the Tootie hits the correct spot, be sure to congratulate him by mentioning that fact. Some students make another error. Instead of breaking the impact by slightly going down in their knees they bounce up which shows lack of appropriate reasoning. To avoid direct teaching you might stop again and give them some practice with 'TTT', which is Tootie Tongue Tracking. You may have noticed that some children use their tongues when writing to help them focus. Have them point their tongue at the Tootie as it rises (until the very last moment). This is a great help. As vision improves children do not need to use their tongue anymore. Pointing with a fingcr also helps improve tracking.

Red-green exercise

This exercise is for children who are already performing on a more advanced level. Ask the child to select a red and a green Tootie and put them on the Launcher. The green Tootie should go on the blinking eye at the end of Launcher, and the red one in front of it. Both Tooties should touch the Launcher and should lay flat and not be on top of each other.

Next to the Launcher on the floor, put a similar pair of red and green Tooties with one of them a little to the right of the other, as shown in the picture on the right. The Tooties on the floor must be in the same sequence as the Tooties on the Launcher.

The Tooties on the floor indicate the color to the right should be caught with the right hand and the other with the left hand. After each try the child should look at the sample on the floor to verify if he has done it right and verbalize the results. Having the two Tooties on the floor showing the right way to catch allows a child to keep checking himself to see if he did it right. The picture on the previous page shows how to catch the Tooties at their 'dead point' at the top of their orbit which is easier as the Tooties stop for a split second before coming down again. However, the only way to be successful catching 15 Tooties at once, as mentioned before, is to catch them on their way down. Some people are quite successful in catching them in a 'sandwich fashion' where they have one hand underneath the stack of flying Tooties and the other hand above. Some children can catch up to nine Tooties this way, so do not show any disapproval if a child does this but be sure to compliment him.

When a child can do this exercise three times or more, fairly easily and without missing, he is ready for the next step. Now he has to try to catch the Tooties three times the opposite way of the example on the floor, again without missing. If necessary you can tell him to change the example on the floor first, as doing it the opposite way might be confusing in the beginning. When getting better the child can keep the example the same after switching and catch the opposite way. If you try this yourself, you will discover that this is quite hard to do as your mind is set to catch one way. Your thinking has to adapt in order to catch the color you were used to catching with the left hand now with the other hand. This technique exercises parts of both sides of the brain very effectively. When the child is ready, have him place any color Tootie between the red and green Tootie on the Launcher, and then take that one away leaving a space of one Tootie width between the red and green Tootie. Have him now catch the Tooties and, when ready, try catching three times in a row without missing. When a child is skilled at this exercise, try catching the other way around. With some practice the child may be able to judge a Tootie width without using a Tootie to measure the middle space. If not sure, he can always put a Tootie in the middle to verify.

It will make him feel good when he is right. It is important to teach children to judge distances and this exercise is perfect for that. Later, separate the two Tooties by two Tootie widths, and repeat. As the space between the two Tooties increases, catching the Tooties will become more difficult but most children should be able to catch them when placed at least three Tootie widths apart.

Most children tend to catch the Tooties after they have reached their high point and are on the way down. But trying to catch them on their way up will be even more challenging when a child becomes really good.

Catching the more 'aggressive' way is a good practice for a child when he has become better in catching. The picture to the right shows how to catch the more aggressive way when the Tooties are still on their way up. Add this to the instruction when the child is ready and willing to make catching the Tooties more difficult.

This means that a child should try to catch the Tootie while it is coming up, and before it has reached the highest point. The hands should be turned down (do not tell) to make catching easier. Remember that a child should be given the opportunity to figure this out on his own, as he needs to learn how to learn. When you get good at it, the aggressive way is more efficient and actually quite easy.

When a child gets better coordinating both sides of his brain, the Tooties can be moved further and further apart. The red Tootie, which is closest to the child, will always come up less high than the green Tootie. Again, as the spacing between the Tooties increases, the catching will become more difficult. Children love to do difficult things when they are not criticized, and they will learn that 'failure' is an essential part of the learning process and can, in fact, be lots of fun.

Learn to laugh at these failures and think of what can be done to do things differently in order to avoid them. When a child has the opportunity to enjoy lots of failures and learn from them, he will be able to see failures coming and can learn to avoid them if desired. Notice that with this exercise the peripheral vision is being stretched. The child should not focus on one Tootie alone but he needs to be able to see both Tooties at once in order to catch both of them. It is a great visual and motor exercise. Changing into the reversed order of catching will teach children to adapt to a new situation and to be more flexible in the use of their minds.

Using a stopwatch to time how long it will take to do a certain exercise, or part of it, will add an additional challenge to any of the Tootie exercises. Have a child do this over and over, as now he can easily see from his chart that he is making progress. He can see this for himself without you having to tell him, which is most important for learning self-esteem.

Tootie Toss

In general, avoid letting new children even see the Tootie Toss. They will prefer it to the Tootie Launcher. All children would rather throw than catch. This may explain why children love to throw stones in lakes and against windows. Even babies standing in a crib love to throw. Allow children to become proficient with the Launcher before exposing them to the Toss. They will then be more willing to go back to the Launcher which is the most useful tool for the basic skill of learning to learn. Do not allow children to throw objects other than Tooties in the net as these objects are likely to bounce back very fast, hit the child or others, and cause injuries. You might want to try a very soft ball, just for fun, but other objects should not be allowed.

Keeping the Toss in place

You might have to hold the Toss while a child is throwing. When you work with a single child this is no problem, as you can observe a child carefully while sitting behind the net. However, when you work with more children at the same time, having weighted bags to keep the Toss in place will be a big help.

It is recommended to sew two bags for each Toss, fill them with sand, and place them on the horizontal legs, as shown on the picture on the next page.

Notice that they are placed close to the net. The cloth should be strong and tightly woven and 17 inches (43 cm) square before you fold it to make the bag. Be sure to fill the bag quite full. When filled as suggested, they will weigh about 10 pounds (4.5 kg). When placed on the horizontal part of the legs, these bags will keep the Toss in place, otherwise it tends to move when a child throws a Tootie hard and fast.

Prevent children from throwing these big bags into the net, as it might break, or the springs might stretch. Either way, the net will lose its tension. Once the springs have been stretched, it is impossible to get them back into shape again. Replacing springs will be the only way to get your Toss into good working condition again. One of the secrets of the Tootie Toss is the tightness of the net to maintain bouncing qualities.

Keep children from throwing the big bags to each other as well. Tooties are filled with special crystals, which shift much faster than sand does and it spreads the load over a larger area. Bags filled with sand (which has a tendency to stick together) will hit a child like a rock. Tooties are safe, as the special crystals shift as soon as it hits a surface. This will prevent children from getting hurt. After the Toss has been used very frequently, or after years of heavy use, the net might stretch a little causing loss of tension. To achieve the best results, the hooks on adjacent sides of the net should be moved one hole inward in order to get the required tension in the net again. For best results, the net must always be quite tight.

If you happen to have king-size Tooties, you can use these to hold the net. King-size Tooties are also great to exhaust hyperactive children when you throw one back and forth to the child.

This will help him to relieve excess energy in a safe and controlled way while exercising his motor skills at the same time. This works much better than telling a child to sit still or be quiet. Telling a child does not teach him how to control himself. The king-size Tooties, Size 10, weigh about 10 lbs (4.5 kg), but can be made heavier or lighter depending on the needs of teachers or therapists. Some size 10 Tooties have been made to weigh only 3.3 lbs (1.5 kg) but it is difficult to make them this light. When lifting any heavy Tooties, or lots of Tooties in a bag, be sure to teach children to use their legs and not their backs. In this case, direct teaching is necessary to avoid injuries.

Positioning of Toss and child

To have Tooties bounce back the right way, please follow the instructions very carefully for best results, as the Toss is a very precise working device.

In the beginning, have a child sit with his back towards a wall, but sitting just far enough away so that he cannot lean against it. Giving a child the opportunity to lean against a wall will make it much more difficult for him to become actively involved. Have the child sit cross legged and put the net close to his legs, but not touching. Another reason for placing the Toss this way is to make sure that if a child throws too hard, the Tootie will hit the wall and no one else in the room. It is important that Tooties do not fly all over the place, possibly hitting things or disturbing other children in the room. As the Toss is a very sensitive tool, it is important to carefully observe the child, as well as the way the Tootie returns. Please take care that the Toss is correctly positioned so the Tootie will hit the child about chest height if not caught. This will prevent children from being afraid of Tooties hitting them in the face.

If the Toss is positioned a few centimeters off in the distance or angled, it can make a big difference. It is important to be aware of this. The positioning of the Toss should also depend on how hard a child throws. If a child throws hard, you might want to consider turning the Toss upside down so that only the long legs touch the floor. In

general, the Tootie returns perpendicular to the net, regardless of the angle it hits the net, unlike a ball when it hits a wall.

The size of the holes in the net and the size of the tooties are designed to work together. Every now and then a Tootie will bounce unpredictably to help keep children alert. This is why it is important to use genuine Tooties to get the desired results.

How to start

Throwing and catching with both hands is the easiest way to begin. Normally developing children will start throwing with one hand and maybe catch with both hands in the beginning, but soon they will want to try to catch with one hand as well. Children with difficulties tend to use both hands simultaneously at first which is best, before advancing to catching with one hand. Less developed children often prove to have difficulties doing one thing with one hand and something else with the other hand.

When catching with both hands the child's body should be facing the center of the net. When using only one hand, this hand and the shoulder should be directed towards the center of the net. Observe if the Tootie always goes over or under the child's hand when he's trying to catch, or if it goes to the side. Also, observe if he does this consistently or randomly.

When he does it consistently, it could be a clue that the child is not problem-solving very well. When the same thing continually goes wrong, the child should be wondering what is happening and what he could do to solve the problem. When errors occur randomly, it could mean the child does not know where his hands should be in space to be able to catch, or that his eyes and hands are not working together very well. You might want to draw his attention to the fact that, when things always go wrong the same way, he might need to think of other ways to attack the problem.

Many people tend to repeatedly make the same mistake without changing their technique. This can be very frustrating as they continue to fail, not finding out why. People then tend to give up as they do not want to continually fail. Therefore, it is important to have children discover how to deal with problems and how to develop mental tools to look for solutions. When children learn to observe more carefully, they learn very valuable skills for solving problems in school and in real life situations in the future.

The best way to start is to have a child throw a Tootie in the net and let him find out what happens. Normally a child, unless he is very young, should be able to figure out, before he throws the Tootie, that the Tootie will bounce back to him. Less developed children might be surprised when the Tootie bounces back. Do not tell the child to catch, but give him many compliments when he starts catching, and even more when he starts to catch the Tootie before it hits his chest.

As you observe some children trying to catch, you will notice that many times the Tootie will pass over the child's hand. Do not tell him, but the most efficient way to catch is with the fingers up and spread out, as shown on the picture at the right. When the fingers are directed down or straight out it is very easy for the Tootie to pass over the child's hand. If the Tootie does land in his hand, he is likely to push the Tootie out of his hand when closing his fingers.

On the other hand, when the fingers are directed up and the tootie lands in his hand, it is natural to close the fingers around it.

If you are patient and encourage the child to continue with appropriate compliments, it is quite likely that while exploring various ways of throwing he will discover a successful manner of throwing with his fingers up.

Observe if a child has both hands fairly close together when catching with both hands, as this is more efficient than having them further apart. Eventually you want the child throwing overhand (fingers up). This is a more natural way of throwing and it is the way toddlers throw from a crib. This is an example of one of the few times you need to teach directly if the child does not eventually discover this by himself.

Catching after the Tootie hits one's chest is very normal with young children, and is observable even with adults. The first few throws might hit the chest, but people with well developed skills will quickly want to catch before. If they tend to be lazy, however, they may be satisfied with letting it hit their chest because it is much easier. At first some children will try to catch the Tootie after it hits their chest which is fine. Be sure to compliment them on this. Do not try to speed up this process by telling children to catch, but by complimenting them when they start trying to catch all by themselves. After a child develops good catching skills using both hands he might make efforts to start catching with one hand. Be sure to compliment him when he makes this effort on his own initiative, and encourage him to continue. If he is good at catching with one hand, have him try to catch with the other hand, which is more difficult.

For more developed children you might want to start with the non-dominant hand first so a child can look forward to easier work with the dominant. Please be patient and do not move to the next level before the child is ready. For a child, *it is a rewarding feeling when he becomes good at something.* Moving on too early will prevent children from the experience of learning to do a task easily and automatically. This is important when children need to learn to do more things simultaneously. When the child is not able to perform physically on an automatic level, too much thinking and concentration is required for a specific activity, leaving less energy to focus on the task itself. Performing various skills simultaneously is required in school. It is, therefore, very important for a child to develop his motor skills to function at an automatic level.

It is best to start throwing with a regular (classic) Tootie (5.3 ounces, 151 grams). If a child catches accurately it will stay in his hands. However, if he tries to catch the Tootie in a careless or uncontrolled fashion it is more likely to bounce out of his hands. Sometimes a Floaty Tootie (2.6 ounces, 75 grams) or a Tweenie Tootie (3.5 ounces, 100 grams) may work better especially for younger children and those who are more afraid. These types of Tooties are lighter and return more gently. But, they are also livelier and more difficult to catch. You have to decide what is best for a particular child. You might even consider using a larger size as these will be easier to catch. A size 3 Floaty Tootie, if available, is suggested as a good start.

Normally a child should want to start catching right away, which is great, and we should compliment him. If a child, however, does not start catching, do not tell him to catch, but praise him for whatever effort you observe. Initially you may need to praise him 'just' for throwing, or 'only' if a child attempts to catch. Even if the Tootie hits a child's hand by accident, be sure to compliment him by telling him it was great he touched it. Show sincere enthusiasm and interest for all small, successful steps in the same manner you would when a child does catch the Tootie.

When a child is ready, tell him to count the number of times the Tootie hits the net regardless if the Tootie was caught or not. You can even time the child and see how many times he can hit the net in three minutes. This will give a child a goal and help him practice counting. Writing down the date, the scores, and how many minutes his trial was, helps a child to see for himself that he is getting better. Later, you can have him time himself to see how many times he can get the Tootie to hit his body without it dropping on the floor. He can count how many times he succeeds in preventing the Tootie from touching the floor. The next step is to count the catches. Providing a child with appropriate goals will help him to achieve them, and gradually he will develop more body control. A child's throws will gradually become more consistent and catching will become easier as well.

Observing how the learning process develops, and enjoying the progress a child makes, will make the process much more interesting for you. Learning how to observe carefully will make you more sensitive to small changes and improvements, and will help you adapt the exercises to meet the needs of each child. You can also observe the gradual development of the learning process as well as the integration of thinking skills, body control and independent learning.

When working with older children and adults, observe if they are aware of when they miss and wonder why the Tootie goes over or under their hands. If their self-generated learning ability is functioning, they should be able to take those clues to alter the placement of their hands. Fluent throwing and catching also depends on how consistent someone is in applying just the right amount of force when throwing, and whether the Tootie hits the net flat or on the narrow end. Be sure to avoid telling children 'the tricks of the trade'.

Complimenting a child is very important, as it gives instant feed back on what he does right. Remember, it is not only what you do, but also how you do it that produces the best results. Children are dependent on us and are very sensitive to how we judge them. We should always keep in mind that this has an enormous psychological effect on them.

Many children, especially children who have difficulties in school, are often told what they do wrong. In order to have them feel good about themselves, gain self-confidence, and learn to focus on what to do instead of what not to do, they need to be told what they do right, instead of continually telling them what they do wrong. *Positive feedback will motivate children to continue and not give up, and motivate them to enjoy the feeling of improvement.* The Tootie teaching method and the Tootie equipment are designed to provide positive feedback right away, but it is essential that the teacher adds his or her own *positive* feedback as well.

Remember, our first goal is not to teach a child to catch, but to allow him to learn on his own, for example, how to throw the Tootie consistently so it hits the chest every time. This will improve his self-generated learning abilities. It is very helpful to have children throw more than 100 times without the Tootie dropping on the floor before advancing to the next level. It also helps to have a child repeat this in future sessions. Again, this will help him learn to count efficiently and provide him with a good feeling for numbers and the quantities they represent. If a child has never experienced how many 100 times is, it will be much more difficult for him to understand the concept of numbers and math. When doing this exercise children with poor motor skills are provided with the chance to count repeatedly. This gives them the opportunity to improve their skills in several areas simultaneously. They also learn to integrate these skills, which is very important. When they reach a more advanced level, the numbers of catches will increase, proving they are getting better. There is a tendency in many schools to push children to a higher level before they have been allowed to establish a firm foundation at a lower level causing them to remain insecure at each higher level. We want to provide them with a good foundation first.

If you observe a child having difficulties visually tracking the Tootie, especially when it bounces back to him, it is a good idea to go back to the Launcher as tracking Tooties being launched is much easier for less-skilled children. The Toss is a great tool for children to exercise their focussing ability from near to far and back.

If possible, the teacher should always be in front of the child to observe the child's eyes. Observing the eyes carefully will gradually make you see the differences in performance from one child to another.

In the beginning, whenever a child misses the Tootie, a new Tootie should always be available immediately. It is best to let a child have a pile of Tooties next to him. We want to achieve as much continuity as possible in throwing and catching so the child does not forget what he did wrong if he misses. In other words, the time interval between a miss and the next throw should be as short as possible. Another exercise is to give a child about 50 Tooties and have him throw them at the net one right after the other. Later, when he has started to catch by himself, tell him to make two piles. One pile will be the Tooties he has caught, whether this is with his body or with his hands, and another pile with the Tooties that touched the floor. One side of the child can be the 'caught' pile and the other side the 'missed' pile. After finishing all 50 throws he should count the number of Tooties on each pile. If a child has difficulties counting, he can put the Tooties end to end in a matrix to see which is bigger. While throwing and catching a child exercises honesty and learns to make decisions quickly as well.

Only when a child has become good at throwing and catching at close range should the Toss be moved further away from him. Later he can also throw while kneeling or standing up. Encourage the child to decide how far away the Toss should be when he kneels or stands.

Catching with eyes closed

Another very good exercise is to have the child throw and catch with his eyes closed. In this way you can observe how the child processes the information he gets through other senses of the body than his eyes. It allows you to see what mental tools the child is using when he does not have input from his eyes. It shows, not only how a child processes the information he hears or senses through the muscles of his body, but also how well he learns from that information.

Other senses now provide input to the brain and the so-called 'internal vision' is developed. Developing proper visual abilities involves understanding what is seen, using the input of other senses as feedback, and processing the information obtained. When a child succeeds in catching with his eyes closed it gives him a feeling of great power. In the beginning, he should be sitting cross legged, close to the net but later the Toss can be moved further away.

This is an excellent way for blind children to learn how to throw and catch. Have the child feel the Tooties, the net and its position first. Ask him what he thinks would happen when he throws a Tootie at the net. This is important to talk about as the child should know what is going to happen, and that there is no need to be afraid. Since normally-sighted children can learn how to throw and catch with their eyes closed, it should be even easier for blind children since they are used to processing information coming in through other senses. You will be surprised to see how easy it becomes for children to throw and catch on an automatic level with either hand. It is important we do not explain or help them once they are confident the Tootie is not going to harm them, even if it should hit them accidentally in their face. Remember that the position of the Toss can be critical for success. There is more information on catching with eyes closed in the upcoming section on 'Throwing with one hand and catching with the other'. When a child is not allowed to open his eyes, it is interesting to observe how inefficient his search can be. A Tootie can be right in front of him, to either side, or even in his lap and some children will have difficulty finding it.

When he is unable to find it with a 'helter skelter' search, a child should learn to think of how he could do it so that none of the space around him is missed. It is common trait of all ages.

When a task seems simple, people use their physical skills and not their whole brain, even after many failures. Trying physical skills first is a good idea for fast results, but when it does not produce the desired results, they should decide to use their brain and mental resources. Observe if they finally become more efficient in searching or if they continue to make the same mistakes again and again. You can also see these same tendencies on the Tootie Launcher. Whether people have their eyes open or closed does not seem to have any effect on the way they use their thinking skills.

Throwing while standing

In the beginning, keeping the same position from which a child throws is very important. Consistent feedback from the same position should be obtained in order to determine what mistakes are made when missing the Tootie. You might want to put some tape or a different color Tootie on the floor to mark the place to stand. The child will be able to come back to the same position after coming back from picking up a Tootie. It is important to observe if one foot is put forward. This foot should be the opposite of the hand throwing. Again, do not tell the child, and observe how long it takes him to discover that this is a more efficient way to throw. Many exercises, as mentioned above, can also be done while standing up. Again, this will give the child a new experience of throwing and catching. Scores on a time sheet will also be interesting. Notice on the picture above that the nets of the two Tootie Tosses are different. The one in the foreground is a custom built Tootie Toss designed to automatically reward the child when he hits the center of the net.

Notice that the centre of the net has a small section of fine mesh netting added to the netting with much larger holes than the standard Tootie Toss. The size of the holes in the outer net are designed so that in about 50% of the throws the Tootie will stick in the net and not return. This tends to give a jolt to the thrower so he avoids hitting the outer section. If you have a standard

Tootie Toss, you can weave a piece of ribbon in the center of the net to encourage the child to hit the centre. You can also weave other shapes in different parts of the net and then tell the child to throw at the circle or triangle, etc. These shapes should be near the center of the net for best results.

Varieties of throwing and catching

There are many ways to use the Toss. If you allow children to experiment, they will show you many ways of using Tooties, some of which might be new to you and useful for other children. An overview of some of the various ways to throw and catch a Tootie follows.

1. The easiest way is to have a child count how many times he can throw at the net. Whether he catches the Tootie or lets it drop on the floor is not important. The goal is to have the child achieve a consistent way of throwing first, before he moves on to a higher level.

2. Once a child is good at throwing, you might want to have him count how many times he can throw at the net during a three-minute time span (or more or less whatever is appropriate to the situation). Have the child time himself and write down his scores. In this way you provide him with a goal and he can see his own improvements. Be sure to have him write down the time and date as well so later he has a written proof of how much he has improved. This way of writing things down will also help him learn how to document. Be sure to save these papers in a safe place. It will be interesting and very rewarding for him to look at them later and see the progress. You may need to help some children with reading the time and doing the writing. Later, you can fold in writing exercises, like writing the numbers down in straight rows and writing neat numbers. When the child has to write down numbers all the time, he gains lots of practice without the pressure of having to solve math problems.

3. Have a child count how many times he can throw at the net without the Tootie touching the floor when he misses. For this exercise, the child is sitting cross legged. If the Tootie lands in his lap or on a leg, it counts as a catch. At this level, it is not important whether he catches directly, or if the Tootie hits his body first. Only when the Tootie touches the

floor should he start counting from one again. Have the child write down the number of catches before he starts again.

4. Count how many times he can catch with both hands without missing. When a child misses, he has to start counting all over again to try for a higher score. Scores should be written down as often as possible so a child has to be able to see his improvements rather hearing it from other people. Having a child count will encourage him to become more determined to catch. At some point he will figure out that he can get much higher scores when he catches the Tootie because this saves time. After a catch he can throw much faster at the net again. This will help him to become much more efficient in his movements, and it will speed up his reactions and thinking abilities, as he has to react instantly to the situation.

5. When appropriate, have a child start a stopwatch before he starts throwing and stop it when he misses. In the beginning the teacher may need to read the time for him. On his paper, he can write the number of catches in column one, and the time it took in column two. Show the more advanced and older children how to use a calculator to calculate the time per catch and write this down in the third column. Later, in the forth column, have him calculate the inverse which is catches per second, but be careful not to do this until a child is ready for the additional challenge. Requiring a heightened skill too soon will stress a child.

6. When a child can achieve high scores while catching with two hands, you might want him to count the times he can catch with one hand. He should be able to catch with one hand easily before increasing the pressure by counting or timing him. Some children tend to fail when there is too much pressure. In this controlled environment with Tooties a child can learn not to be afraid of failure or pressure. With Tooties there are no consequences like failing an exam. Most of the time children exhibit their own ways of reacting to failure or pressure which actually can limit them and cause part of the problems. Often, it is not the pressure that causes problems, but the way the child reacts to the pressure. When he learns to deal with this he has made a lot of progress.

7. When a child has gained some proficiency start moving the Toss further away, and repeat all of these exercises again. Having the net further away will give a child a different expe-

rience of throwing and catching. Since the Tootie takes more time to bounce back to him, this will have an effect on the number of throws and catches within a three-minute time span.

8. Throwing with one hand and catching with the other is a more advanced level of these exercises. Here a child has to pass the Tootie from the catching hand to the one that will now do the throwing. It gives him a good sense of the left and right part of his body, and helps him to cross his middle line. When he becomes good at this, he can start counting and writing down his scores. Timing himself is the next step.

9. When a child is comfortable throwing and catching this way, have him throw and catch the other way around. This will be more difficult again, but he will learn to change from a comfortable situation into something difficult. This can be a fun exercise, as it is very challenging. Throwing and catching will gradually become a rhythmic movement and will give the child the feeling that he can go on without stopping. This gives children a feeling of confidence.

10. Now you can go back and repeat some of the exercises using a metronome, for example, and have him throw in time with the rhythm. Allow him to set his own speed on the counter and speed up when he can.

11. All of the above listed exercises can be done with the eyes closed as well. Catching with the eyes closed is easier when a child sits close to the net. It is preferable that the thrower does not open his eyes to find the missed Tootie but do allow the child to peek in the beginning until his confidence improves. Try to give in as little as possible without putting pressure on the child. Many children search very inefficiently. If it is clearly out of range you can help them by using the terms 'hot' and 'cold' to indicate if the child is close or far away from the object. This method can also indicate how a child is listening or hearing. If they repeatedly search on the wrong side, you might want to have his hearing evaluated. Children who make the same mistakes repeatedly tend to not use their thinking skills to analyze a problem. For some children, advancing to the level where he is not allowed to peek at all can be too much in the beginning.

12. The next step could be to have a child kneel or stand in front of the net, and repeat the various exercises as described above.

Now the position and angle have changed and responses will have to be adjusted. Catching with the eyes closed becomes more difficult the further the child is away from the net, as well as when a child stands. For some children it might be a challenge to try anyway.

13. Again, give children the freedom to experiment every now and then. They will discover more ways of using the Toss than you have thought of, and you can learn from them as well.

Teaching self control

For some children it might be advisable to purposely not position them in front of a wall as mentioned before. There are situations in which you might want to consider doing it the other way around, for example, if children have problems controlling themselves. The room, however, should be suitable for this exercise. Avoid having other children in the vicinity who might be disturbed while doing their own exercises. Put away things that might be knocked over if a child throws too hard. Just give the child a few Tooties and see what happens. If hc is sitting and the Tooties go beyond him, he has to get up to retrieve them. With time he should get the message that, if he controls himself and the amount of force he is using, he saves himself a lot of work and effort. Such children who do not control themselves are also likely to waste time and energy in real life. Therefore, for some children this could be a very important learning exercise.

It is advisable not to do this exercise in the beginning, but there might be situations, for example, with very hyperactive children, when you want to do it this way anyway.

Normally, we want a child to gain confidence in throwing first. Always remember that, when you teach directly and tell a child how to do something, the learning opportunity is lost. The secret is to allow a child to start mastering control from within. This way of teaching is very effective in helping a child learn how to control himself. Children can apply this control in other situations as well. We want to support and maintain this way of learning at a subconscious level to keep it as effective as possible.

Having a child time himself can be a big help as well, as he will discover how much time he is wasting by uncontrolled throwing and having to retrieve the Tooties all the time. We have to find indirect ways to encourage a child to start to control himself. This is what we are looking for.

Once control has been mastered by experience with Tooties, a child will be able to transfer this to other situations. This is very important as parents or teachers will not be around to correct him all the time. Tooties will show him how inefficient he is, and he will become motivated to change. Often, the actual problem is not visible or clear to a child. Just by telling him 'to concentrate', does not mean he knows exactly what he should concentrate on or focus on, especially if he has never had the experience. Exercising body control with Tooties and indirect teaching will be a big help to him, and to people around him.

Throwing from one person to the other

One way to have two children use one Toss is to have them throw and catch to each other. One child throws and the other one catches the Tootie. The catcher then throws the Tootie back to the other child by way of the Toss. Since the Tooties are designed to usually return perpendicular to the net, both children should stand fairly close to a line perpendicular to the net as shown in the picture at the left. The Tootie will return to the middle of the space between them.

Another way is to have the catcher throw the Tootie to the thrower directly. Later, reverse the order with the other child throwing. In this way, the catcher should remain near the perpendicular line, but the other child may be off to one side at about 45° or more.

The next step is to have two nets. The children throw at the same time in each other's net and catch the Tootie thrown by the other child.

Do not tell them that throwing at the same time makes it easier and lets them continue without having to wait for each other.

This is a great way to learn to work together. Teamwork and communication is important to learn.

Running and catching

This exercise works well with a number of children, for example five, just as well as with one. Position the Toss at some place in the middle of the room and anchor it down with large Tooties, as described in a previous section, or have one child hold it. Each of the children takes one Tootie in his hand and lines up. The distance from the net can be adjusted to the level of skills of the group.

With a piece of tape, mark a certain spot from which the children should throw. If too many children go past the spot, it shows they are insecure in their throwing so you might want to make a spot closer with a different color or number. From that spot the children throw their Tootie at the net. As the Tootie usually bounces straight back from the net, the children have to run to catch the Tootie.

All the children, one after the other, can now throw their Tootie (fast) at the net, run, catch, and get back in line again. If they miss, have a pile of Tooties available near the end of the line so they will not block others as they would if they tried to retrieve the Tootie they missed. Later, the missed Tooties can be picked up. Observing how the missed Tooties lay on the floor can give you an idea as to how many children missed the net, did not throw hard enough, or could not catch.

If you have more Tosses available, then you can put more nets at a distance from each other. After throwing and catching at one net, the child does the same at the next Toss, and then the next. An alternate suggestion would be to divide the children into groups of various skill levels for each net with the throwing point closer for less-skilled children. This way, children are running in big circles around the nets. Each time they are at the throwing point near the front of the net, they throw, catch, and then continue running. This can be done outdoors as well as in a big room such as one for physical education. All exercises can be adjusted to a larger group of children. Just make the circle big enough so they do not get in each other's way when trying to retrieve the missed Tootie. It is best to have extra Tooties available so they do not have to retrieve the missed ones until later.

Spinning exercise

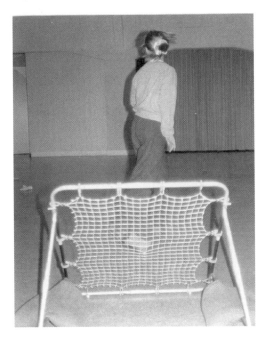

In this exercise the child has to throw the Tootie in the net, spin around, and catch it. This is an advanced level exercise and most of the time best suitable for older children.

It is wonderful to have pictures to show children. Notice that the picture to the left was taken at the exact moment that the tootie hit the net. If you have a digital camera, you have to press the button just before the tootie hits the net.

With most digital cameras you should focus on the net by pressing the shutter release button half way down and then all the way down just before the Tootie hits the net. It is wonderful to have pictures to show the children. Observe which way the child spins, as one direction is generally more efficient. If the child is using his right hand to throw, a spin to the left is more efficient and vice versa. Again, do not correct, as the child might be able to do it the hard way to discover much later that he was less efficient.

Prone exercise

Have the child lie face down so he has to lift up his head and upper body to throw and catch. This exercise will strengthen the neck and back muscles, as well as give children a different awareness of space and their own body movements. Needless to say, this exercise is also good to improve breathing abilities.

Posterior exercise

This exercise, as shown here, encourages the child to do sit-ups and strengthen many muscles. It gives children another awareness of three-dimensional space and how to orientate, as well as to provide another fun way to practice visual tracking abilities.

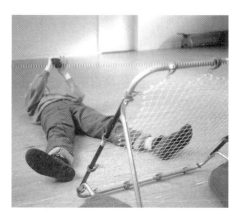 

Tootie Bounce

With the Tootie Bounce, the Tootie can be bounced vertically. Notice the frame held horizontally with one hand on each side about one third of the way up. The best way to hold the Tootie Bounce is with the round red sticker close to the belly button of the child so that he can read the label that says Tootie Bounce. This way, the Bounce can best distribute the force, especially when bouncing a Tootie 5 to 30 meters (16 to 100 feet) outdoors.

The Tootie should bounce a little above eye level so while tracking it, the eyes have to move quickly and remain focussed.

Do not tell the child this but lead him into discovering it on his own. Several skills have to work together, such as holding the net level, using the right amount of force, being alert and reacting quickly, as well as incorporating rapid visual tracking skills. A considerable amount of body control is also needed to make the Tootie bounce consistently.

In the beginning keeping the frame level so the Tootie bounces straight up can be difficult for many children. After some practice they will become better and their bounces more consistent.

To maintain the best bouncing quality, the rubber bands should be changed regularly. They are made out of natural rubber so they age relatively quickly. If not changed in time, such as every three months or more often depending on use, the edges of the net can tear, as more weight has to be handled by fewer rubber bands that remain unbroken. Be sure to store your extra rubber bands in an airtight plastic bag in a cool, dark place.

The regular Classic Tootie is the best one to use in the beginning as this is the most stable Tootie. When they are ready children can try other Tooties as well. Some of Tooties are 'livelier' than others, and therefore, more difficult to bounce. When going for high tosses, such as those going over 5 to 30 meters (16 to 100 feet), it is best to use a Floaty Tootie because this one is more durable if it hits the ground at a high speed when missed.

While using the Bounce the child must be able to move around. Therefore, it is important to use the Bounce in a room with enough space to do so. Less skilled children will not be able to bounce the Tootie straight up in the beginning so it is important to prepare the room so things cannot be knocked down. Using the Bounce is excellent for eye tracking and crossing-the-midline exercises. It is very valuable for visual training and is also lots of fun.

Incorporating timing exercises, similar to the ones described in the Toss chapter, is also very valuable. And, remember, it is important to write the scores down.

Bounce with balloon

This exercise is very good for children with poor motor and visual-motor control. For these children, tracking the Tootie when using the Launcher can be too difficult, as too much speed is involved. Bouncing and tracking a Tootie will probably also be too difficult. Some children are unable to react fast enough to bounce the Tootie several times without missing. When working with children who are not able to track or catch a Tootie after launching, it is very important to have the child practice visual tracking skills using the Bounce with a balloon. The movements of the balloon are slow and smooth and therefore much easier to track than a Tootie.

Make the balloon move a little slower or faster by putting in more or less air. The less air, the smaller the balloon will be and the faster it will go. Putting more air in will slow down the speed but be aware that it can burst easier and frighten a child. If this does happen, it may be important to take the time to help the child overcome his fear by letting him burst a number of small balloons with a pin. If you have a soft fluff ball, try that as the 'flying' speed is in between a balloon and a Tootie.

Some children will want to do this for hours, and they should be given the opportunity to do so, as practicing for hours is often what they need. The problem is that we, as adults, frequently lack enough patience, and we get bored ourselves. However, we should learn to enjoy watching children make progress. Therapists might consider loaning or renting equipment to their clients. Regular practice at home makes therapy more effective.

It is advisable to work with more than one child at the same time so you can give other children attention while one child is doing this exercise (or another exercise) for a long time. Children with coordination difficulties can practice holding the Bounce horizontally as a preparation for advancing to the next level. All children love to bounce a balloon, but after a while children who are more active find a Tootie more interesting and challenging.

Poorly developed visual-motor skills in children are often not undiagnosed. In many cases this can contribute to learning difficulties. These children love bouncing the balloon because it is something they can do, and they enjoy doing it. While practicing and playing children are exercising the muscles controlling eye movements as well as practicing spatial awareness skills. After sufficient time they are ready to advance to the next level.

The way to hold the Bounce while bouncing a balloon is less critical then bouncing a Tootie. Balloons are less sensitive. Holding the Bounce as shown on the picture on the previous page should be permitted, but when using a Tootie the hands should be on each side one third of the way up.

Tootie Bounce for young children

For children up to eight years old, but especially for those between three and six years old, use the Bounce as shown in the picture at the right, above. Have one child sit on the floor cross legged and hold the Bounce at a 45° angle to the floor while the other child throws the Tootie in the net. In the beginning, it is acceptable if the Tootie is not caught but just bounces against the chest or into the lap of the child (as in the top photo on page 79). Avoid telling children that the Tootie should be caught. After some time they will start doing this by themselves.

When working with a group of children such as in a classroom, tell one child to throw the Tootie 10 times. Then the Bounce can be passed to the next person so he can throw. If children throw too hard, they have to retrieve the Tootie themselves. It is important not to retrieve it for them. In this way we help children become responsible for their own actions.

Holding the Bounce with another person encourages teamwork, and bouncing the Tootie this way is great fun. Two children can hold the Bounce and bounce either a balloon or a Tootie. When working with children with coordination difficulties the teacher can hold the net with the child. This way the teacher has control over the

net and can help the child bounce the Tootie or a balloon.

Bouncing a balloon with someone else is not only great fun but it is a very valuable vision exercise for children with difficulties in the visual-motor area as well. As you help the child bouncing, the movement of the hands is being guided, and more attention can be given to following the balloon with the eyes. For children with many difficulties it is often difficult to do two things at the same time. In this way, we can keep the child involved and exercising without overloading him.

This exercise is also valuable for people who have lost some function in their arms or hands. While guiding them through the movements, the paralysed body parts are being exercised, as well as the other parts of the body, the eyes and the brain.

Bouncing a Tootie back and forth

The Bounce is very useful for two children to learn to work together. For this exercise, each child has a Bounce. They bounce a Tootie back and forth to each other. They have to learn to use the right amount of force, and to bounce the Tootie in such a way that the other child is able to reach the Tootie and bounce it back.

Children learn that their partner is dependent on how they bounce the Tootie in order to bounce it back again. This way each child is dependent on the other. If a child bounces the Tootie too high or too hard, the other child will probably not be able to reach it. A series of successful returns is dependent on how each child bounces the Tootie back.

When working in a team the achievements of one person will be influenced by the actions of the other, making people dependent on each other. This is an important lesson to learn in life. Avoid telling this to children, as this concept should be grasped on a subconscious level.

When children can stand further away from each other, such as outdoors, the bounce can be held in front of the face. This way more speed can be generated and there is more freedom to move around quickly.

Standing and holding the Bounce vertically is also a great way for children to learn how to work together. Each child is given a

Tootie, and the teacher gently bounces it back as each child takes a turn. Some degree of controlling force is required from the person holding the Bounce.

When a child is holds the Bounce there is a tendency to bounce the Tootie back too hard in the beginning, so keep this in mind.

When children are more experienced in controlling force and speed, they can challenge each other and have fun. But, in the beginning, the guidance of the teacher is needed. This technique is used for professional baseball teams, but there the Tootie is returned at about 90 miles per hour. Normally you start with a lighter Tootie such as a Floaty Tootie, before moving to a Classic Tootie.

If a child is holding the net, tell him to keep it in front of his face. Another child, standing at a distance, throws the Tootie at the net. The child holding the Bounce can see through the net where the Tootie goes and bounce it back to the thrower. In the beginning it is important to tell the child holding the net, to keep his arms stretched. In this way, he protects his face and prevents the Tootie or the frame from hitting him. When a child knows what to expect and feels comfortable bouncing the Tootie back, more freedom holding the Bounce can be allowed. Once the Tootie has been successfully returned, the thrower can catch the Tootie and throw again. Another idea is to have more children throw and catch. Now children have to line up and go to the back of the line after throwing. By changing the angle of the Bounce slightly, the child (or adult) holding the Bounce can make catching for the other child easier or harder.

For parents, teachers, or therapists, it is good to operate the Bounce this way, as you can decide how much or how little you want to help a child in the beginning.

For children who are having difficulties, you can 'help' the child by aiming the Tootie into their hands at chest level, or give a little more speed when they do not throw hard enough.

For overly active children aim the Tootie in such a way that the child has to run or jump thus helping him get rid of surplus energy.

Tootie Bounce outdoors

When the Bounce is used outside, the Tootie can be bounced very high. It is best to use a Floaty Tootie when trying to bounce as high as possible. The Classic Tootie is heavier, and therefore more difficult to bounce very high. When the outdoor surface is hard, like concrete or brick, there is a chance that the heavier Classic Tootie will break because of the immense force of hitting the ground if a child misses it.

By bouncing the Floaty Tooties very high, more active and even hyperactive or aggressive children can get rid of surplus energy very quickly in a controlled, safe and fun way.

For children, as well as adults, it is very challenging to try to bounce the Tootie as high as possible and as many times as possible. Do not tell children, but the secret is to bounce the Tootie vertically and keep the sun behind their backs.

Have another child use a stopwatch to measure the time of each trial and to record the time and the number of bounces in a tabular form. Children love timing each other, and it encourages them to want to become better.

Bouncing between Bounce and Toss

This is a great exercise for older or more skilled children. It is great fun and challenging to keep the Tootie bouncing back and forth.

The closer the Bounce is held to the Toss, the faster the Tootie will go. Standing further away will make the exercise increasingly difficult. Here is another opportunity to time each trial.

Exercises with only Tooties

It is recommended to have children help you count all the Tooties before you start working. Counting Tooties serves various purposes. One is to make children aware of the value of the Tooties and also that you have a definite number of them. When children help count them again at the end of the lesson any missing Tooties can be found. Sometimes they drop behind radiators or curtains, and it might even happen that a child loves them so much he cannot resist slipping one into his pocket.

Last, but not least important, children gain continuous experience in counting and at the same time become aware of quantities and the value of numbers which is very important in learning math. Many children are not able to visualize how many 50 or 100 is. If they have the opportunity to count Tooties many times, it helps them to get an essential feeling for numbers and quantities. Too many children have reduced opportunities to experience different numbers related to quantities when they come to school, and this frequently continues during the learning process later.

A proven way for children of all ages to learn about quantities is to have children lay 10 Tooties end to end in a row. Arrange 10 rows of 10 Tooties together to make 100. Leave a space for the next rows of 10 until you have another 100 Tooties. This gives a child the experience of counting by 10's and 100's and makes structured numbers and the metric system visible. Very few children have ever seen numbers related to quantities like this before.

Another alternative is to have children lay five Tooties end to end in a row. Have them arrange five rows together to make 25 and leave a space before they arrange the next 25, as shown on the picture at the previous page. It makes counting the Tooties easy and it is another great math exercise for children. In this way, many math problems can be made visible as well, which is a great help for children to learn to understand math concepts. Playing with Tooties and learning this way is fun and motivating, and the most beautiful thing is that they do not realize they are actually learning math. This approach is especially good for children who have become afraid of solving math problems. Gradually math can be brought to a more abstract level, while guiding children without the need of being afraid. More suggestions on using Tooties to learn math will be given later on.

Tootie road

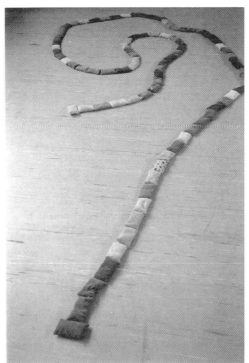

Children up to about 12 years old like to build roads and play with Tooties as pictured on the right. Resist any temptation to tell them how to build the road and allow them to experiment and make their own discoveries. Later you can ask them why they built the road the way they did. This helps develop children's language skills. When a child is ready, you may suggest some alternatives, such as all Tooties must touch, or perhaps that no two Tooties of the same color should be next to each other, etc. Roads can curve to go around tables and chairs and go from one room to another.

Ten Tooties end to end equal one meter. They can help children to get a feel for distances. Tooties are mathematically designed so precisely that three Tooties end to end also equal one foot. When children are ready for it, have them count the number of Tooties by one's or two's, and then divide by 10 (for meters) or three (for feet) to get the number of meters or feet. For many reasons it is recommended to have a supply of about 200 Tooties or more. The feeling of distance needs to be developed on a subconscious level first, for example by making Tootie roads. Then Tooties can be used to learn to estimate and visualize distances and later apply these skills in a task.

Variations

- Make a road from wall to wall. Alternate laying Tooties flat and on the edge, or straight and crossed.

- Make a road with Tooties side by side to make the road wider, and therefore easier to walk on (for example for children with poor balance skills).

- Have a child make a perfectly straight road. Use a stretched string to test its straightness. Take away the string and have the child adjust the row until he thinks it is perfectly straight. Then test again with the string and repeat until the row is perfect. This is a great way to exercise vision and accuracy. Children should be allowed to do this exercise many times until they are good at making perfect rows.

- Build roads with right angles.

- As children get better, add patterning and some cognitive tasks. Ask children to make the road in such a way that no two Tooties of the same color can touch each other. Another option is to lay down patterns such as having two Tooties of the same color, followed by two or more Tooties of a different color between them. Try sequencing colors such as red, green, yellow, etc.

- Ask children if they can think of other ways to build roads. Let children experiment, as they will become creative and try many different ways using their imagination.

Tootie walk

Have a child take off his shoes and socks and walk over the road he has made. This is a great way to give road building a different meaning. Another very important reason is that the child practices balancing in a safe way. For children who have poor balancing skills, it can be frightening to walk on a wooden balance beam because they may be afraid of falling and hurting themselves.

Walking over a Tootie road is safe and children can feel free to practice and enjoy it.

In addition, Tooties feel great to walk on, a little like walking over the soft sand of the beach except Tooties provide a steady underground.

For children with poor balancing skills, you might want to have them build rows of Tooties side by side first. This makes wider roads and gives a child more space to walk on in

the beginning. When a child becomes better and more balanced, make roads of Tooties end to end. Some children feel the road is too narrow and they build roads of Tooties side by side by themselves. This shows great thinking ability. Be sure to give them a compliment as it shows the child is learning and solving problems by himself. This is what we are looking for!

Tootie circle

Have a child practice making perfect circles. In the beginning, use old bicycle tires or hoops as guides until the child becomes very good. Have him lay the Tooties on the outside or the inside of the guide. When the circle is finished, the guide should be carefully removed and the child gets to see what a perfect Tootie circle should look like. Later, when a child is very good at this, he can try to make circles without the guide and check himself by putting the guide in or around his own circle when finished. This gives a child a reference to check. If the circle is not perfectly round, have him take the guide out, make corrections and put the guide back in to check. In this way, a child learns to be precise in laying the Tooties. For all children it is important to

learn to be neat and precise, as many mistakes are caused by sloppiness. This can be very frustrating for children if they are not aware of this. Learning to be neat and see the benefits of it will be of great help to these children. It is very important for children to have plenty of opportunities to learn by checking themselves and by making corrections until they have become used to it. When learning at school, children are expected to do this all the time, but some of them do not know how.

Once children have had the experience, they will be able to apply this skill in other situations as well. If possible, have bicycle tires of different sizes or find other materials, which can be used as a reference. When a child is very good at making circles, he can start making them bigger and bigger without using a guide until he is ready to make a circle of about 50 Tooties. For more advanced children, place a meter stick on the floor and ask the child to make a circle around it. If necessary, use several meter sticks laid out on the floor like the spokes of a wheel.

Have a child walk over the circles, forward and if possible, backward as well. When he is very good at this, he can start trying to do the same walk but with his eyes closed. This will be much more challenging and difficult, as our vision, as well as our reference point at the horizon, is normally used to help keep our balance. If a child is not ready to make a circle without assistance, help him a little and make one together, as he will still practice laying the Tooties neatly and see what a circle looks like. Walking over it will be very rewarding, and as already said, provides good balance practice. When ready, start encouraging him to make one without any help.

Tootie crawl

This exercise is very valuable, especially for children at the crawling stage. Put a Tootie on their back or head and have them crawl around the room and, when ready, to a specific destination and back. Then try adding more Tooties. Even when a child is at the walking stage already, it is still valuable to do these exercises because you can observe their crawling pattern, which should be cross lateral. Put a Tootie on his head, or let him do it, and have him crawl to a specific point and back. Congratulate him when successful and then add a second Tootie laid criss-cross, and repeat. As more Tooties are added, children naturally tend to be more cautious. Children who are not cautious should learn this because they need to learn to adapt to changing circumstances. It is interesting to observe what happens when there are many children crawling around. They need to be aware of their space and not bump into each other.

This exercise is useful even with older children and young adults. It helps them gain body awareness, concentration, and a feeling for how their body has to be moved without the Tooties falling off. Later lay one or more Tooties on a child's head and, when he is ready, on both his head and his back. The next step is to have the child put the Tootie(s) on his head himself. Putting the Tooties on his back himself may be too difficult for a young child, so you might have to help, but let them try first. This valuable exercise seems so simple but most children still love to do it, especially less skilled children. It is something they can do and it is fun to put more Tooties on their head and challenge them to become better.

Crawling race: Have children carry 10 or more Tooties on their backs to the other side of the room as fast as possible. Begin with one Tootie at a time, transport it to the other side of the room and put it at a designated point. The child then returns to collect another Tootie and transports it again, etc. To increase the degree of difficulty let the child gradually transport two, then three, then four Tooties at a time. Gradually increase to 10 or more Tooties if the child is skilled enough. It is always a good idea to have children (when ready) race against time so they can see when they get better. A record can be kept in each child's workbook. When ready, a child can write down his own time.

If a child cannot write yet, do it for him until he can do it himself. Racing against time prevents slow children from always being the loser. It is important to have them discover they do get better with practice. The positive feedback when they see better scores shows them they can win, and win more often. This will encourage them to continue to improve, instead of always losing races. Children with many difficulties are most likely to always come in last. However, they are the ones who need practice the most, and you want to prevent them from giving up or being disappointed with themselves.

Little children can be encouraged to pretend to be different animals, for example a 'camel' with two bumps or be a 'mule' carrying his packages through the desert. Use your imagination to extend the infinite possibilities.

Tootie towers

Building a tower as high as possible is a very challenging exercise for all ages, even for adults. It requires concentration, neatness, care, visual skills, as well as thinking and learning skills.

Needless to say developing these skills is very important to other learning situations, especially in school. Start with one Tootie on the floor and put the next Tootie criss-cross on top of the first one. After adding another Tootie to the tower, the tower should be able to stand by itself without the child holding it, before adding the next Tootie.

If the tower falls over, the child has to again try to build a tower of the same height or higher. It is important to be flexible in the beginning. As long as the child is learning, concentrating and thinking, we should let him continue but add new instructions when he is ready.

To document the progress it is important to have a child write down the height of his tower each time. After some practice, children who have become skilled will discover that the tower is much more solid when the heavier Tooties are on the bottom and the lighter ones are on top. It is also very important to make the Tooties as flat as possible and stack them as neatly as possible to make the tower more stable. Never tell children or demonstrate, but let them discover themselves, as this is important for developing their self-generated learning abilities.

There are various ways of building towers. The criss-cross ones and parallel ones (shown in the picture on the right) are very popular. Keeping towers up is usually difficult after stacking 17 Tooties but some skilled students can go up to 30 or more.

At any age, it is a challenge to build towers. On the picture at right, Sofie (on the left) shows the very special tower she invented. When there are plenty of Tooties available, children can become creative and all kinds of structures and towers can be built. It is not only great fun but very good for learning body

control, concentration, as well as learning to be precise and persistent. For building a single tower (on the right) as shown on this same picture (previous page), the same skills are needed to build it as high as it is.

Building a tower with Tooties on the edge (picture above left) gives an interesting structure.

Also try building a tower using a double-width (picture above right). Building a tower placing Tooties in a double-width pattern is great for small children and children who are not good at building single towers yet. Towers built this way can become much higher as they are more stable.

Tootie hop

Learning to jump is very important and Tootie towers are great for practicing this skill. Nowadays, more and more children who do not know how to move their bodies efficiently in order to jump off the floor can be observed in classrooms. If they are not able to do simple things like this, imagine what happens if they have to do more complicated things in school or later in life. Teaching them to jump is a first step to making children more aware of their bodies.

Running in circles and then jumping over several Tootie towers is also a very good exercise for learning body movement. It is a very important vision exercise as well. Children have to learn to estimate distances to each tower of Tooties, as well as estimate how high they are, in order to be able to keep running and jumping without knocking them over.

For less skilled children, it is important to start at the lowest level and have them line up, for example 10 single Tooties with a good distance in between. Then have them jump over the Tooties without touching them. In the beginning, they can even just step over them to give them self-confidence and practice their visual skills. Let them practice until they are good at this and feel confident, and then advance to the jumping level. When ready, have them make towers of two Tooties on top of each other and jump over them. The higher the towers get, the more difficult it becomes, and it is a great challenge for children to see how high they can get. Have the more skilled children jump over towers with their feet together. Let them count how many times they can jump over them without knocking one over. You could start having them make a tower of three Tooties, and jump over it 10 times. Then add one Tootie to the Tower, and have them jump 10 times again, and so on. When the tower falls over, children have to build it up and try again.

When successful after 10 jumps they are allowed to add one more Tootie. To make it even more challenging have children put a Tootie between their ankles and jump without dropping it. This exercise gives them muscular feedback as to whether they keep their feet together or not. Have children write down the results of their achievements, as it is important for them to have a written proof of their improvements. Another fun exercise is to have children sort the Tooties by color and ask them to build towers of all one color. If there are, for example, more green Tooties than red and yellow ones, children will have to build towers of various heights. They can place them at various distances from each other as well. This will give them a different experience again as now they have to learn to adapt to these various heights and estimate the distances.

Variations:

- Have children build different types of towers: criss-cross, parallel, and 'on-edge'. Jump over each of them.

- Jump over the towers with a Tootie between a child's knees or under his arms.

- Step over the towers with one or more Tooties on a child's head.

- Instead of you thinking of different variations, it is always better to have a child think of other ways, and encourage him to explore and be creative.

Even though these exercises sometimes may seem boring to us, children like to do them very much. These exercises will give them plenty of opportunities to learn to jump and control their bodies and vision. Building towers provides valuable vision and concentration exercises as well as teaching children to be neat and precise. This is what they need to become good learners, and to practice using their body and mind working together.

Tootie structures

Children love to make all kinds of fantasy figures, houses, castles and streets using Tooties. They are very safe and even when the highest structure falls over, no one needs to be afraid of getting hurt. Tooties, therefore, are great to have, especially in day-care centers and nursery schools. Playing with wooden blocks gives another very different and important experience to children. However, they can be a threat to some children, especially those who are afraid or insecure. Most likely they will be the ones reluctant to experiment, even though they need the experience of building and experimenting even more than other children.

Building activities are important for children to practice creativeness, vision skills, and to learn how to plan and structure. These skills are essential for learning at school. A child needs many repeated experiences making plans for things he would like to build.

Learning to think how he is going to start, and how he is going to proceed in order to get done what he has planned, is essential and adds to his problem-solving skills. Many children have great but unrealistic plans, or do not know how to do things in an organized way to implement their plans. Some children do not have the experience of planning and structuring at all and have very little feel for what is a realistic goal. These exercises help children learn to use their brains to gain insight and practical understanding in real life situations, as well as to learn the first simple laws of gravity and physics. Later, these skills can be applied in more abstract learning situations in school. Children greatly need these experiences, as later on it might be very difficult for them to structure and plan on an abstract level in higher grades.

An example of experimenting making figures is the 'ballerina' (top of page 96) made by a seven-year-old boy who loved to make it every time he came in for therapy. Parents and teachers should allow all children to experiment making figures as long as they like, even though many adults might find this activity not appropriate for older children. If a child continues to show

an interest in making these figures and structures, allow him to continue. It is very likely that he is still learning something. Once a child does not learn any more by doing a certain activity, he will stop and find another one, and advance to the next level all by himself.

The tower in the picture on the left is a very interesting one to build.

Building an igloo is, for many children, a very interesting and challenging exercise. Have them start with a small circle of Tooties about 18 inches or 45 cm in diameter. The next layer is just a little bit smaller than the first one, and so forth, until the igloo can be closed with a few Tooties on top. The test if the igloo has been built properly, is to have the child sit on it. If the structure is built correctly, the igloo will easily hold the weight of the child or even of an adult. It is very rewarding for a child when finally he has been able to build one that can hold his own weight.

You might want to assist the child to carefully sit on the igloo while holding his hands so he feels secure. While still holding his hands, a further test of his igloo's strength is to have him lift his legs so that his entire weight is on the igloo. It is lots of fun if it gives way, so encourage laughter and give him the opportunity to build a stronger one as many times as he wishes. One of the secrets of building a strong igloo is to have the joints overlap with the next layer like bricks in a wall, but do not tell this to children. An igloo that starts out with a circle of about 18 inches in diameter gives the best results but requires about 150 Tooties. Start with a smaller circle if you do not have enough Tooties.

After a child is able to build igloos successfully, add an interesting math experience. This time take a piece of paper and record in tabular form the number of Tooties in each layer and then the total number of Tooties. Have a child assume that each Tootie weighs 5.25 ounces (151 grams). Make another column for the weight of each layer and finally the total weight.

While all Tooties appear to be the same, except for color, they can be quite different in weight. For this exercise, we are concerned only with the weight, so on the next igloo use a scale to weigh each of the Tooties before the child puts them in a layer. Record the actual total weight of each layer and the actual final total weight.

Children love to experiment building with Tooties. The more Tooties you have, the better. If you allow them to experiment, you will sometimes see fantastic structures like the tower on the previous page. Therefore, it is very important not to tell children too much of what to do or how to do it as this will hinder their own creativity. We need to teach children to use their own brain and imagination instead of having them do the things exactly as teachers or parents have in mind. This is very important in helping children to become independent people who can think themselves!!

If you find that your children really enjoy building projects with Tooties, increase your supply. They take up very little storage space. Children love putting them away by tossing them into a large container on wheels. In most cases, allow children to keep their structures for several days and make pictures of them.

Tooties in a basket

This is a valuable exercise not only for younger children but for older children as well. Have a child sit on the floor and give him a number of Tooties (30-50). In the beginning set the basket a short distance from the child for him to throw as many Tooties in as possible. Have him count how many he got in.

Give the child enough time to achieve this and have him repeat as many times as needed to become very good. After improvement, gradually move the basket further away. In this exercise children learn to use their eyes together, to focus their eyes at various distances, and to learn to control the right amount of force needed to successfully throw a Tootie at different distances. Needless to say, children also practice their ability to throw overhand as well as underhand. Underhand can be quite difficult while seated depending on the distance to the basket.

When a child is very good and has reached a consistent throw, ask him to stand at a distance from the basket that is easy for him and try to throw a Tootie in the basket. When he has gained a certain level of proficiency he can try to do this with his eyes closed. Now he has to be able to judge sound clues and tell from hearing where the Tootie went. Have him verbalize after every throw if he thinks he was successful, or if he thinks the Tootie went beyond the basket, or if it did not go far enough. Allow a child to check after every throw to see if he was right or wrong, and have him verbalise the results. It is a great feeling for a child to say when he is right. In the beginning, he may think it is impossible to do. However, it will give a child a rewarding feeling to see that he can do things he thought would be impossible, and that practice and persistence helps him to be successful. After some practice children gain proficiency which helps build their self confidence. Later, a child can try to throw from further distances, and while sitting on the floor as well.

The next step is to give a child a number of Tooties and let him try to throw them into the basket with his eyes closed and without opening his eyes between the throws. After finishing all the Tooties, he can count and see how many he got into the basket. Have him practice keeping the same distance and see if he is able to get more into the basket every time. Again, it is important to have a child document the results to have written proof of his progress. It is also interesting to use baskets of different heights and let a child discover that he has to adapt his throws to this new situation.

Tootie jump

Tootie jumping exercises are another way to give children a lot of jumping practice and provide them with more experiences to develop body aware- ness. Start with one Tootie under the armpit and have them jump, for example, 10 times. Then change sides and hold the Tootie under the other armpit. Other useful activities are to have children hold the Tootie in the crook of each elbow, between their chin and shoulder, on their tummy, on their knees, between their knees and ankles, etc.

When holding a Tootie in the crook of their knee children have to jump on one leg. Each way gives a child an opportunity to jump 10 times. Most children with learning difficulties also have poor body awareness and find jumping difficult to do. It is amazing how difficult some of these exercises can be even though they seem to be so simple to us.

Helping these children to learn to control their bodies by using their brains will provide them with essential skills to do much better in school. They learn how to move their bodies and use their sensory input to be able to do what they want or need to do. Jumping and holding one Tootie is the easiest way to start. Later you can add another Tootie and have them hold two Tooties on various parts of their body, for example, one under an armpit and one between their knees, etc. A much harder exercise for many children is to hold a Tootie under their chin and jump 10 or 25 times without dropping it.

These exercises are very powerful, even though they appear to be quite simple. They can be particularly hard for children with motor difficulties. In each classroom there are children who have trouble simply jumping off the floor. The power of the Tooties method is to start with simple things first, and allow children to become very good before advancing to the next level.

This jumping exercises provide a solid basis to build on. If you are a classroom teacher, you can easily have your children do this exercise in the morning before you start class. They are not only very useful exercises but they help children breathe better, as well as make them more awake and alert, a perfect way to start your teaching day. The best way is to plan a variety of ways of jumping, working from the head all the way down to the feet. This way, almost any child can be motivated to do hundreds of jumps. If you would tell a class of children that they have to jump 200 times, they most likely would not want to do it, but with the Tootie jump exercises, it is possible to lead them into jumping that many times without realizing it.

As already mentioned, if you look at a classroom full of children, you will still find many of them who do not know how to move their bodies as efficiently as they should. They have difficulty doing these exercises. They have more difficulty moving their when one small part of the body seems occupied or 'locked'. It is very difficult for them to move one body part independently from another part.

It is very interesting to observe children follow instructions, especially in the beginning. You will see children who have diffi-culty following instructions precisely even with relatively simple tasks. Now you know why these children might have difficulties during a lesson. They miss essential parts of your teaching and end up not knowing what to do. Using simple tasks like these jumping exercises help children to learn to pay attention and follow instructions precisely. This is invaluable in keeping up with the learning process at school. These exercises can also be combined with the Tootie hop exercises to provide you with a big variety of jumping exercises.

Catching Tooties with closed eyes

This is a very valuable and effective exercise to use in classrooms before starting lessons in the morning or when children are restless and are having trouble concentrating.

The best way to start is to have children put a Tootie on their head, cup their hands, and hold them against their belly button. The only instruction is to move their body in such a way so they can catch the Tootie. In the beginning, you might allow children to move their hands away from their body, but when they become better they are not allowed to move their hands away from their tummy to catch the Tootie. Let children try as many times as necessary so they become good at it.

The next step is to have them do this exercise with their eyes closed. Sometimes it can be useful to start with their eyes closed first. They will have a much better feeling when they are successful than when they start with their eyes open. It also teaches children that they are able to do difficult things after practicing and not giving up.

The next step is to have children cup their hands behind their back and catch the Tootie. They will feel very proud when they can achieve this as well, as it seems to be hard in the beginning.

Again, it is sometimes best to do this exercise with their eyes closed first (even though they cannot see the Tootie). The exercise improves their visualization process and it helps to improve concentration.

Tootie distance guess

Have the child throw a Tootie some distance away from where he stands and have him guess how many steps it will take to walk to it. Of course, this will depend on how big he will make his steps, but let him discover himself. Ask him to count each step aloud. You want to observe the learning process that is taking place as well as his abilities to reason and to count. Soon he will learn if his guess was right, too high, or too low. Let the child return to the same spot and repeat until he gains proficiency in estimating distances.

You will see children unable to reason very well. They do not seem to realize that if they continually throw to the same spot and it takes, for example, nine steps to walk to the Tootie, then the next time it will also take the same nine steps to get to it. When a child continually throws the Tootie to another place on the floor he will have to adapt his guesses to the changing circumstances. Do not directly tell children this because it is essential they discover it by themselves. This process of reasoning is very important in the learning process. It is also a very valuable aid to vision development.

Later, have children walk heel-to-toe (putting one foot right in front of the other) and estimate and count how many times their feet will fit in that distance to the Tootie. They have to figure out that the size of their feet is smaller than the size of their steps.

In the beginning, it is a good idea to always throw from the same spot so the child learns to use the same objects in the room as a reference. This will help him to use his vision more effectively as well as help estimate distance as accurately as possible. When he is ready, gradually begin to change the starting point. The child can try many different sizes of steps, or even hops, and estimate how many big steps, small steps, or normal ones it will take to get to the Tootie. He can also measure how many of his foot lengths it will take from the starting point to the Tootie. These exercises will help a child to develop a good sense for distances and numbers, as well as practice his reasoning and vision skills. This is another very good exercise for learning to adapt to changing circumstances.

If you do not help children and let them learn by themselves, you will most likely observe them do things beyond your imagination. Many times the difficulties these children face are overlooked because it is assumed that these skills develop naturally and are mastered without much effort. There are children, however, who simply can not master these basic skills. There are children who do not realize that if you are at one spot in the room and you throw a Tootie close to the wall, for example, that it will take so and so many steps to get there. If the Tootie is thrown again from the same starting point and the Tootie lands near the previous spot close to the wall, it will again take about the same number of steps to get there. It is hard to imagine this could be very difficult for children in the beginning. Either they just make wild guesses without using much reasoning, or they have very little awareness of numbers and distances. If this exercise is difficult, it is likely that numbers have very little meaning to the child. Imagine how difficult solving math problems must be for them. There should be no need to explain that learning about numbers and quantities by direct experiences, as described above and further on in this manual, is very important to a child's under-standing. These experiences will provide them with references for future and more complicated math problems.

Standing up and sitting down

Have the children sit on the floor and place a Tootie on their heads. Now ask them to stand up and sit down again without the Tootie falling. In the beginning, you may allow them to use their hands but later, when they are very good at this, they can practice not using their hands at all. Sometimes you may want to start

without using the hands so you can observe how each child goes about solving this problem.

Children feel good when they finally figure it out. This is an excellent exercise to develop intense concentration and body control for all ages because of the instant feedback. In the beginning, many children will move too fast with too little control, or they sit down too hard making the Tootie bounce off their head. Children will have to discover that the smoother their movements are, the better the Tootie stays on their head. Gradually children will start to move more cautiously and adapt to changing circumstances.

When a child can do this easily with one Tootie, he is allowed to put a second Tootie criss-crossed over the first Tootie to see if he can do the same with an additional Tootie on his head. The child learns to realize that the higher the tower on his head becomes, the more carefully and concentrated he has to move. Again, avoid telling children this. Remember that we always want to allow children to learn to think for themselves. We want them to learn to use their reasoning, as well as learn how to have their body and brain work together.

The most difficult part of this exercise is when children are sitting down. At this point movement is more difficult to control. When the child can do one level five times successfully without failing, for example, he is allowed to add another Tootie to the tower on his head. For most children, and even adults, this exercise becomes difficult with a tower of six Tooties or more. The picture on the previous page shows how concentrated a child must be to succeed. If concentration is experienced through movement first, a child will become much better at concentrating using his mind alone, as needed in the learning process in school and in other situations later in life. Learning how to solve problems by using sensory input, reasoning and common sense is essential. The experience can be transferred to other situations if learned the right way.

Throwing a Tootie under one's leg and catching it

Even though this exercise seems to be simple, it is a very powerful and important one because the whole body, as well as the eyes, is exercised. The child learns how to move his body and use his eyes in order to catch a Tootie this way. The left and the right side of the body, and combinations of left and right, are used. This enables the child will to become very aware of left and right and it helps him to learn how to cross his midline. The best way to start is to ask the child to throw a Tootie under his leg up towards the ceiling or up in the air. Do not tell him to catch it as this might be too difficult for him in the beginning. For children with poor body control it will be especially difficult to aim the Tootie towards the ceiling, or even to figure out how to do this. Sometimes they cannot figure out how to move their body efficiently and they do not come up with the idea that they should lift one leg and throw under it from the outside. The girl in the picture on the previous page is throwing the Tootie from the inside.

This is more difficult because the child has to be able to cross his midline. Many of children do not even know how to lift their leg properly and keep their balance. Catching may seem an impossible task to do in the beginning. It is important to encourage children to simply aim towards the ceiling as a first step, or have someone hold the Bounce over their head as a target. Initially it might be important to have children throw a Tootie up in the air with their hands and catch it first before advancing to throwing it under their leg.

Allow a child to decide for himself which leg he prefers to throw the Tootie under and which hand is easiest to use. Do not give any suggestions but just observe what he does and which preferences he chooses. Give the child time to really become good at each level. Have him count the throws so you can hear him counting. In the beginning have him count without starting over after the Tootie has dropped on the floor, as starting over might frustrate a child if he is not ready for a higher level of skill. When he is very good at throwing and catching, have him count the throws and start over after he misses. Be sure to tell the child that starting over is not a punishment, but a chance to improve and become better. Have the child write down his scores after each trial and number them so he can see for himself that he is getting better. This way, he also learns to count, and the better he gets the more practice he has counting.

When he is ready, ask the child to use his right hand to throw under his right leg and catch with his right hand again. The right part of the body is being exercised intensively now. When he is very good at this, have him switch to throwing with his right hand under his left leg and catch with his right hand. Later he can throw with his left hand under his left leg and catch with his left hand. Catching with the throwing hand is more difficult for most people. There are various ways of combining the throwing and catching sides of the body.

It is possible to make this exercise even more interesting, challenging and useful when you have the child lay as many Tooties on the floor, as the number of catches he makes without missing. Let us say a child successfully catches two times in a row. You then ask the child to lay two Tooties on the floor, end to end. If during the next attempt, he catches, for example, five times without missing, he is allowed to add five Tooties to the row already on the floor and so on. For each number of catches without missing, the child adds the corresponding number of Tooties. Have the child start a new row after every 10 Tooties. All rows should be next to each other, touching and starting at the same height. After 10 rows of 10 Tooties, leave an open space and continue with the next matrix of 100 Tooties. This will give the child the opportunity to see how the decimal system is built.

It is important to ask the child every time (if he is ready for it), how many Tooties he will have on the floor after adding the amount equal to the number of catches. For example, "How many did you manage to catch this time?", "How many do you have on the floor already?", "When you add these Tooties, how many will you have on the floor then?" It is very important to have a child check himself and have him count the Tooties aloud each time until he is very sure about his answers. At some point, he will discover it is much easier and faster to use math. Now he only has to count the number of rows of 10, multiply by 10 and just add the single ones of the last row. This is much easier than counting the Tooties one by one again. After discovering this, a child is ready to apply the knowledge to other situations where using math is easier and faster than counting. Experiences like this are very important to motivate children to like math and see the benefits.

This is what a child needs: practice and the chance to count again and again until he is very good at it and until he gains an understanding of what numbers and quantities really are. Only after having fully mastered these skills will the child be able to understand the concept of using math and numbers.

Using Tooties this way is very powerful, as we are able to integrate math exercises while also exercising the body and brain. Teaching math this way will build the self-esteem of a child, as now he only advances to the next level when ready and after a full understanding of what is happening.

If you allow a child to experiment and express his own ideas, he will find more ways to use Tooties for creating new math problems. Children can be very creative if given the opportunity. Experimenting or actually wanting to do something else to avoid coping with a problem, however, should never be allowed as an escape. Many children will start pretending to experiment when they actually want to avoid doing something or when they think they will not be able to accomplish certain tasks. For more math exercises using Tooties, please check the 'Tooties for learning math' chapter.

Jumping with a Tootie on one's head

The following exercise is very useful as a lead-up exercise and can be done with one child or with many children in a classroom. You can easily have children do it (as it is a lot of fun) even if you do not do the next exercise.

Each child is asked to put a Tootie on his head while standing and make one hop so that the Tootie leaves the head at a distance of about one inch or 2.5 cm. Repeat until the child is able to hop without the Tootie falling off or even moving very much. Now have the child or children in the classroom do it 10 times in a row but between each jump, they must stop. This will give them time to contemplate where the Tootie is on their head and how they should jump so it will not fall off, but preferably land back on the center of their head. Soon children will be quite good at it.

Catching a Tootie on one's head

For children who are very good at throwing and catching a Tootie under their leg, alter the exercise and have them throw a Tootie

under their leg and catch it on their head. At first, tell them it just has to hit their head. Children from 8 years and older should be able to do this after some practice.

A good preparation for this exercise is to put one Tootie on the Launcher and catch it on the head, as explained in the Launcher chapter. The secret is that the child throws or launches the Tootie just high enough, so that the dead point is just a little bit over his head. This is the point where the Tootie stops for a split second before it falls down. This is the perfect moment to put the head underneath and have the Tootie land on it. It is very important not to tell a child but to let him practice and find out for himself. The best Tootie for this exercise is a Classic Tootie as this one is more stable and heavier than a Floaty Tootie which will tend to bounce off the head. Many children age 8 and over are able to do this, and after gaining proficiency, they can do it 10 times in a row without missing. For some children it might be easier to put the Tootie on their toe and toss it up to catch on their head. Even more difficult is to catch a second Tootie on top of the first.

Passing exercise

Have two children stand against each other back to back. Start by giving them one Tootie and have them pass the Tootie to each other any way they like. Observe how they do this. When it is easy for them, make the exercise more difficult by passing the Tootie over one's shoulder or head and then between the legs of both of them, for example. You can find other ways to make it more difficult. Children have to communicate to do this exercise efficiently. They can time themselves to see how many times they can do this in one or two minutes and get

better all the time. Wanting to become faster will help them to become more efficient.

The next step is to give children one Tootie each to pass on to each other at the same time. This means that when one Tootie is passed over the shoulder, the second one has to be passed between the legs simultaneously. This seems very difficult at first. Do not give them any advice but encourage them to explore. They should find out the best way by themselves. Communicating verbally is one of the secrets. If there is no proper communication, they will have difficulties, as they cannot see each other. Learning to communicate to get this done is a very valuable experience as many things going on between people can go wrong if they do not know how to communicate and understand each other.

Throwing to each other

This is also a valuable exercise for children or adults to learn to work together in pairs, and to pay attention to what the other person needs. It is advisable to have children do this only after they are able to throw and aim properly.

Start by throwing one Tootie to each other and catch. In the beginning, children have to stand relatively close to each other until they are good enough to widen the space between them, making this exercise gradually more difficult. You can also have children throw or catch with the hand opposite to the one with which they started. This will be harder as with the opposite hand, the throws and catches do become more difficult to control. Children have to learn to be considerate when the other person fails.

When they are good at throwing and catching with one Tootie, give each person one. Now they can try to throw a Tootie to each other at the same time. After getting good at this, they can also practice clapping their hands once before catching, and later try how many times they can clap in between. The further away they are from each other the more difficult the throwing and catching will be, but the more times they will be able to clap.

Tootie from the back

This is a fun exercise for children who can throw and catch well enough, and it will challenge them to try other ways of throwing and catching as well. For children with poor motor skills this exercise is still too difficult and it will frustrate them. We want to avoid this. Ask the child to throw a Tootie from behind his back, over his shoulder and catch it in front of him. In the beginning, just throwing from behind his back and over his shoulder can be very challenging. Catching is not important at this stage, so you might ask him to have the Tootie land in front of him. Once the child becomes good at throwing this way and the Tootie goes over his shoulder (and not against his back or to the side), he can start  to focus on aiming properly in order to be able to catch. Again, do not tell him, but let him find out by himself. This is a great vision training exercise, as the child has to visually acquire the Tootie in space and then track it. Catching with one hand or with a specified hand (such as only with the left hand) as well as changing to the opposite hand will make this exercise more difficult.

Catching from the back of one's hands

This is a high level exercise for children who have already become very good at throwing and catching. Give the child two Tooties of different colors. Have him lay the Tooties on the back of each hand and stretch his arms out at shoulder level. Now the child has to pull back his hands fast from underneath the Tooties, and catch them without turning his hands palm up or lifting the Tooties up in the air.

Encourage the child to do this first with eyes closed, even though it will initially seem to be impossible to do. Please note that this is only possible to accomplish when the hands are pulled straight back. When the Tooties are lifted up it is much more difficult because the child cannot see where they go. Please note that we do not say this is impossible, as some children might manage to do it anyway. When the hands are pulled straight back and fast enough, the Tooties tend to stay in place in the air. The only thing the child has to do is to grab back in the same place and catch the Tooties.

When the child is able to catch with his eyes closed he will have a great feeling of confidence and power. That is one of our goals in teaching. When the child is able to be consistently successful with his eyes closed, you might want to ask him to do it with eyes open. This will give him the feeling that this is easy to do but it may be more difficult because with his eyes open his intense concentration might diminish.

The next step is to catch the Tooties with the hand opposite the initial starting-position. It is a great feeling when a child is finally able to do this. It also helps build his self-confidence and teaches him not to give up. It is important to always keep the same color on the same hand when starting so he can be sure he has caught them with his opposite hands.

Throwing and catching on one's back

This exercise will give a child a completely different experience of space and body use. It is an example of how creative one can be in discovering new ways to practice and challenge a child to experiment and have fun. The secret is to throw vertically so it is easier to catch, but do avoid telling the child. Let him discover

Even though this can be done with only one Tootie it is better to give a child about 30, so he does not have to get up when he tosses the Tootie out of catching range. It might be preferable to start this exercise with the child standing up and tossing the Tootie up. It is easiest with an underhand toss.

After a few successes, ask if the child is able to barely touch the ceiling. Be sure the ceiling does not have particles that can fall off if the Tootie hits the ceiling. This exercise requires control of direction, as well as control of the amount of force needed to get very close to the ceiling but not hit it. If it does hit, it should be a very gentle touch with hardly any noise. After the child has become good while standing, he can try it while kneeling. Now he has to adjust the amount of force. When ready, have the child do the same thing while lying on his back, as shown on the picture above. In this position, it usually is easier with an overhand throw. Here is another time when a supply of Tooties is helpful for a child to practice throwing vertically. This is a very valuable exercise because children can learn control of direction and force. Repeat this activity with Tooties of different weights.

Tootie rain

Tootie rain is great for children to learn to respond to things that are happening to them. First of all a child has to be confident in knowing what is going to happen. In the beginning be sure to aim on his chest, or even lower, so the Tootie will not hit the child in the face. You can ask the child if he is ready for the Tootie to drop. The child now can try to push the Tootie away or even catch it if he can. When the child is confident, you might want to hold up a number of Tooties and have them drop one after the other.

Later, speed this up. You can even move your hands so the Tootie will drop on various body parts of the child. It is great fun for the child to react to this and see if the child can push the Tootie away and learn to protect himself.

Another alternative is to ask a child to cup his hands and hold them where he predicts the Tootie will drop. This is a great vision exercise and teaches spatial awareness.

Tootie race

Two or more children can have a race. It is even better is to have two groups of children, each with their own Tooties. The idea is to move a row of about 30 Tooties from one wall to the other while running after each other. Have children start with their Tooties in a row at one end of the room, and give them a fixed point to finish, depending on how far you want them to go. Consider the distance you want children to run. The opposite wall may be too far away, for example, in rooms used for physical education.

While children are running, they always have to move the last Tootie to the front and then run back to pick up the next Tootie. Each child can pick up only one Tootie at a time. Some may want to be more efficient and pick several Tooties, but this idea defeats the purpose of this fun exercise.

Later you can have children run around an object, making the running distance longer if you want. When they have a feeling of how to do this exercise in an organized way, you can use a stopwatch, and have them write the times down. Have them practice going faster and faster. Writing the times down will help them see that they are getting better each time, and it will motivate them to get faster. Trying to remember the times might not be sufficient. Children tend to forget and start relying on you.

We want to teach them how to rely on themselves instead of on other people. If the floor is slippery, have children take off their socks or wear shoes if the shoes are suitable for running.

If you want to repeat this exercise daily, it is important to keep the groups the same and have them try to get better scores than the day before. In this way, each group competes with themselves and not with other groups. Competing against each other does not serve a useful purpose, as the more skilled children will win all the time and the others will always lose which is very discouraging. The skilled children will tend to try not to have the less skilled ones in their group as they slow the group down. When the group has to compete against itself the children will have to work better as a group. The faster children need to keep the slower children involved and improving which is better for the group. Insist on children giving each other positive encouragements instead of scolding each other. This turns this exercise into a social lesson as well.

Tooties for learning math

Children can learn math concepts with Tooties while being unaware that they are actually learning math skills. Tooties can be a very important tool to teach math to all children, and especially to those who have been failing. Many children fear failure which makes understanding math even more difficult. With Tooties math becomes a fun challenge rather than a threat, and children gradually lose their fear and regain their confidence. Numbers by themselves are often too vague for children who have difficulty visualizing and understanding the concepts. Tooties invite children to feel, touch, manipulate and count. This provides them with many experiences of combining numbers and quantities.

Tooties give us many opportunities to make math visible by allowing children to experience adding, subtracting, multiplying and dividing while playing. Learning about percentages is much easier when you can make this visible and meaningful by using 100 Tooties and having children subtract 20% or add 50%.

This way, children actually see what is happening. Explain that 'per cent' means 'per hundred' and when you take 20% you actually take 20 from 100, you have taken 20%. When you want to explain how much 20% of 200 will be, have a child take 20 from each of two matrixes of 100 Tooties. He will see and experience that he ends up having 40 Tooties. Once a child has fully grasped the concept of percentages this way, it will be much easier to solve other percentage problems, as now he can visualize what is happening. First manipulating Tooties to make the problem visible will allow you to gradually move on to an abstract level.

Tooties can be used in many ways and with children you can become creative and have lots of fun. It would be too time consuming to describe all the different possibilities of using Tooties in this manual, but a few examples will lead you to new ideas. If you have enough Tooties available and encourage children to experiment, they will start learning math themselves. Be sure children are able to count properly first.

One of the secrets of Tooties is quantity; the more the better. Try to have at least 100 for lower grade classrooms and even more when advancing to higher numbers. It is very important to give children repeated opportunities to make math concepts visible and to practice enough so they are good at it before advancing to the next level.

The next step is to have children solve a simple math problem in their heads first, and then lay out the Tooties to show if they were right or wrong. Gradually make the problems more difficult. It is very important to allow children to check this way, as this will strengthen their self-confidence. When children are ready, and fully understand how to manipulate numbers when visible, they will not need Tooties anymore. They will become able to solve the problems in their heads alone.

In the picture below, children are grouping Tooties in sets of 10 with a 2x5 matrix, making a road they can walk over when

finished. They are learning teamwork as well as learning from each other. Having children teach each other is equally important to all participants. While these exercises have been designed to work with Tooties, many exercises can be used with other objects as well, such as beans, peas, playing cards, seashells etc. If you have Tooties, the results can be much better, as the Tooties are inviting to touch, and they are easy to manipulate and to put in a matrix. At the same time they teach many other things such as discrimination of weight, sound and touch. Identical looking Tooties can be very different, so they enhance the learning opportunities of the children and make the experience fun in many ways.

Counting while exercising children's motor skills is very important, as explained in previous chapters. It gives a child the real experience of knowing how many 50 jumps are. Direct experience adds meaning to numbers and developing concepts which is extremely important. By practicing many times the child will have experienced counting with his whole body, instead of just on a mental level. Being able to count perfectly on an automatic level is essential for learning math. Repetition is very important where mastering skills is involved. Mental learning alone tends to have less meaning to a child resulting in his quickly forgetting what he has been exposed to. Children need the experiences, not just exposure! What a child has heard yesterday can be lost overnight and not be remembered today. Once the body feels and meaningfully 'knows this knowledge,' it can be turned into a skill that will be remembered in the same way a child learns to ride a bike. Once a child can do this, he can even do it after 20 years without practice.

Structuring as a preparation to learn math

To begin, ask children to group a large number of Tooties in such a way that they will be easy to count. In the picture below, you can see that counting Tooties would be difficult because of poor grouping. The concept of grouping is very important in learning math. To ensure better understanding this should be very clear to children. Children discover that there are many ways of grouping the same number of Tooties. They can make rows of 10 or rows of five and group these rows together again. Allow children to explore and discover these possi-

bilitics all by themselves. This is what real learning is about–giving meaning to math and numbers. Understanding math is much easier if you have been able to see quantities and can apply numbers in real life situations first.

The picture on the left shows children grouping in threes, but they still have not grasped the concept of lining up the Tooties neatly. The picture shows that the Tooties would still be difficult to count.

Teachers may be surprised when 12-year-old children still have difficulties counting to 10 when they are given 100 Tooties or more. When they are asked to quickly line them up in rows of 10, teachers often discover that some of the rows contain less than 10, or sometimes more.

As the sizes of Tooties are all precisely the same, they can be arranged in many different ways such as a matrix of 25 (as shown in picture on the left). While making rows and groups, children will discover counting is much easier when the rows are neat and straight. When the Tooties are laid out in a sloppy way it is much more difficult to see a structure, and it makes easy counting much more difficult or even impossible. This teaches children that being neat is very useful and important, especially in math. Learning to work in a structured manner is equally important. Many math problems are likely to develop when children are sloppy and are not used to checking to see if their results seem reasonable. Many children do not see the value of being neat. Tooties teach them that being neat is important and mistakes can be avoided. This is very important for all children to learn, as many children lack the ability to know how to attack a problem or to think and act in a structured way.

It is very important to teach children to continually check themselves in order to determine if they are right or wrong. This affects their self-esteem as well as their newly developing skills. A teacher telling them whether they are right or wrong is not enough. Children need to learn by doing it themselves, and seeing it for themselves. If wrong, they need to check to find out where it went wrong. If right, children can feel very proud, as they have now learned to take charge and check for themselves. Many children who have learning problems have had very few opportunities to experience this.

If a child has little understanding of basic math concepts, it is often not clear where, or how, to search for the problem. Children need to understand the concept and the process well enough so they 'can stand on their own two feet' and not rely on others.

Making math problems visible

Grouping small quantities of Tooties shows children how to group a fixed number. Ten Tooties can be grouped in various ways like 9+1, 3+7, etc. However they are grouped the total will always equal 10.

The picture at right shows three towers of four Tooties. The child can see and verify by audibly counting that 3x4=12. Sorting Tooties by color and counting how many there are of each color can be the subject of various interesting math problems.

Adding becomes more interesting and meaningful when a child has to add a number of red and green Tooties. Many different groups of Tooties can be created and the child can now add all the numbers of different colors and check the result by counting the Tooties. A good way to give children the experience of subtracting is to give them some Tooties to count. Then have a child take out, for example, all the yellow ones and count these. The child can then count the Tooties that are left. These kinds of exercises provide many opportunities to learn to see what subtracting really means.

As shown in the picture on the left, the result of having 12 Tooties divided by three is easier to understand when the child places the Tooties into three groups. When the Tooties are all the same color, it is better to leave a little space between each row. The results are easier to see. After children have been given a lot of time sorting and grouping Tooties, they are ready for exercises. They can make groups and write down the math problem that goes with the grouping. When making 10 groups of two Tooties, children write down 10x2 =20. They then count the Tooties to check if the problem and the answer they wrote down agree. They can also do it the other way around and group the Tooties first, write down the math problem they have created, plus the answer, and check if they did it correctly. They create their own math problems and write them down.

Grouping the way this picture shows, makes it visible to the child that 16÷4=4 or 4x4=16, depending on how you want to present the problem. Grouping 100 Tooties in many different ways is a very useful exercise also, as many children cannot visualize how much 100 is. When children group Tooties many times in many

different ways, they learn to use their vision and gain experience through movement before being confronted with a mental exercise alone. This makes grouping much easier to visualize later, when math problems have to be solved in children's heads alone. The important skills of visual and tactual discrimination are used to learn complex concepts.

Weighing exercises

In order to learn it is very important for children to gain more awareness of their surroundings. Learning about weights shows children the differences between heavy and light, as well as the various qualities of materials. Some things may appear to be heavy, while they actually are not, and the other way around. The only thing we need to do to encourage curiosity is to provide children with opportunities. Weighing things is one of these. Children love to look around and find lots of different things to weigh.

The first step is to find a scale with a needle because we want the child to grasp the concept of how a scale works without going into scientific details. For a child who has to grasp the concept of weighing these details are not of much value yet. We just want to provide the experience of watching the needle going further down the heavier an object is. For learning purposes, old scales as shown in the picture to the right are the best ones as they tend to make a sound when something is put on it. Why this is important is explained later on. The best way for learning by experience is to set the scale on a table and have the child find something to weigh, such as a toy, a book or kitchen item. He has to put each object on the scale and see what happens. Normally, the child should be able to observe that the needle moves down. We should not explain what is happening but have the child find other things to weigh and lead him to discover that as the objects get heavier, the further down the needle drops. When the child has some under-

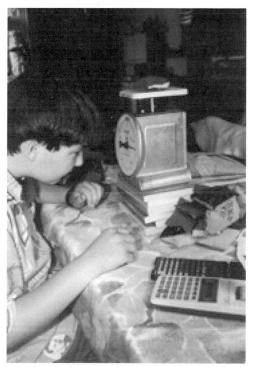

standing of numbers, he will find out that the numbers on the scale indicate the weight.

When he is ready, explain that the little marks indicate the grams and the bigger marks, the kilos, or ounces and pounds depending on the country you are in.

Children who easily grasp this or have gained an understanding of weights can find many things and make a list of the items with their corresponding weights. Using an analogue scale first is very important as the child can actually see that the weight is pushing the tray of the scale down and the needle is reacting to this. When the child is proficient in weighing this way, a digital scale can be added. Now the child weighs an item with the analogue scale first and then puts it on the digital scale to see what happens. The child will see that the digital scale will indicate about the same weight but now in numbers. A child should be able to transfer his knowledge from the analogue scale into an understanding that a digital scale indicates the same weight but now with numbers going up instead of the needle going down. If the first step (using an analogue scale) is missed, it might be more difficult for a child to really grasp the concept of weighing. It might be more difficult to for him to understand how a digital scale works, and what is shown on the display. It is very important to give a child the opportunity to learn by experience, as this will encourage him to become curious and explore, and therefore learn even more. He might wonder if there are differences in weights, or if it might be possible that there is even more to discover about various materials or temperatures, etc. This is adding to the development of self-generated learning abilities of a child.

The next step is to have a child try to predict the weight of the object before placing it on the scale. It is so rewarding when a child becomes sensitive to weights and he finds out that his guesses get closer, or are even precise at times. This will make him become more sensitive to small differences and improve his ability to discriminate. Being able to predict what is going to happen is a very valuable learning tool. A child gains insight to the first, simple laws of physics, providing him with more under-standing of the world around him.

Since Tooties are very versatile they can also be used for weighing exercises. They create very valuable learning experiences as it is possible to raise the level of difficulty very easily.

Learning to sort and organize, as explained earlier, are very important skills in the learning process. It is important for a child to become sensitive to small changes or differences. As already mentioned, start using Tooties to learn about weights by using an analogue scale. If you cannot find an old one that makes a noise, try to find a new one with a needle. The one making the most noise is to be preferred.

Start with a pile of Tooties and see if the child is sensitive to the various weights. If you have not done any sorting activities yet, ask the child to sort the Tooties in any way he wants. Probably he will start sorting them by color as this is the obvious way for most children. Compliment the child for  doing this and count how many different colored Tooties there are. When the child is proficient in sorting this way, the next step is to ask the child if he can think of another way to sort the Tooties. If he can not come up with another way, ask the child to close his eyes, feel the Tooties, and then ask him if he can feel any differences. Depending on what the child comes up with, ask him to sort the Tooties by feel or sound, and have him verbalize what he thinks the differences are.

Give a child as many different tasks as necessary to lead him to the discovery that there are differences in weight as well. Once he has discovered this, he can start grouping the Tooties by weight, and make different piles of Tooties of about the same weight. When all Tooties are sorted and piled, use the analogue scale to check if he was right or wrong, and have him verbalize the result for each Tootie. Then, he can make two piles of Tooties, one of the piles for the ones he judged correctly and the other pile to show which ones he misjudged. It is very important to give children many opportunities to do this exercise so they become good at discriminating various weights.

This also builds self-esteem. The two piles will show him if he is getting better, and he can be proud when the pile with the wrong ones gets smaller and the other grows.

When a child is good at discriminating, we can add another degree of difficulty to the exercise. This time ask the child to put a Tootie on the scale as delicately as possible. The goal is to not have the scale make any noise at all and to take care that the needle does not wiggle but slowly moves down until it stops. When you do not have a scale that makes noise, just ask the child to make the needle move down slowly without wiggling. This is a very powerful exercise for children who have difficulties controlling force and it will help them to learn to concentrate. They have to be able to guide their movements very carefully and this kind of scale will give them instant feedback. At the same time, the child is learning about numbers related to real situations. Do not comment or correct them when the scale does make noise or when the needle wiggles. But, do compliment them when they are successful. This is much more motivating as the child can easily see when something goes wrong and he will be more motivated and happy when we recognize his progress and genuinely compliment him.

The next step is to ask the child to put the Tootie on the scale with one hand very carefully, verbalize the weight and write it down in tabular form. Then have him take the Tootie off the scale just as carefully with the other hand. When taking the Tootie off, the scale should not make any noise either, nor should the needle wiggle. In this way, the child learns to have the left and right parts of his body work together and still be in control. At the same time he is exercising concentration, vision, and his ability to focus as well as gaining motor control. By adding a new task when the child is ready, he learns to concentrate and pay attention to several things at the same time. Once he can do this with Tooties, he can transfer these abilities to other situations in school and in real life situations. And, we have allowed him to learn how to use his mind in order to stay in control of a situation.

The next step is to give a child a pile of 30 unsorted Tooties. Now he has to estimate how much each Tootie weighs and verbalize his guess. Next, he puts the Tootie on the scale delicately, verbalizes the weight and, then, whether he was right or wrong. Using a tabular format, the child writes 1 (for the first Tootie to weigh), his guess (e.g. 80 grams,) the actual weight of the Tootie (e.g. 100 grams) and yes or no (for right or wrong). Later, another column can be added where the child has to calculate how much he was off. This teaches him to use math. Next, he carefully takes the Tootie off with the other hand. A chart that can be used for documenting the results in the beginning is included in the back of the manual. But, when the child is ready he should use a piece of paper with lines and practice making straight rows without the guidance of a tabular form. Now the child learns to structure and do things in a certain sequence as well as to document, be focussed and concentrated, control his force from within, and be neat and careful.

Now try a digital scale. The child has to add another column to the chart or on his piece of paper, write down the weights from both scales in the two columns, and check if they agree. This will add another activity to the sequence and make it more difficult, giving him more things to think of. It will give him a lot of experience in reading digital numbers and comparing them with the analogue reading for a full understanding. Children need a lot of repetition to be able to master certain skills. If he has made a mistake when reading the numbers on either scale, this will come out and he has to check again. When the weights of both scales match, he can pile the Tooties on the right side. In the last column the child can write down how many grams he was off with his guess. If suitable to the situation, have a child mark his close guesses with green and the ones that are far off with red. On the paper it will show if his marks are mostly green or red, and the next time he can try to come closer with his estimates.

When the child has mastered this level sufficiently, tell him that after weighing the Tooties, he can build towers, instead of just making a pile.

When he has, for example, a pile of 30 Tooties on the left side, he has to go through the whole sequence again, as described. When he is ready, he takes the Tootie off with his right hand very carefully again, and starts building a tower. Depending on what he chooses, he can make towers of five, seven, 10, or even more, whatever is suitable. Let him discover that he has to leave space for other towers. In the beginning he just might start to build without thinking whether the other ones will have enough space. This will help him learn to plan, to predict when he is going to create difficulties for himself, and to avoid these by using his mind and thinking skills. It will help him expand his sequencing abilities, concentration span and motor control, including vision, and thus perform more efficiently. Later, he can try building higher towers.

For children who cannot read the clock yet, it can be very useful to set a clock on the table and have the child observe how the hands are moving. It is helpful to mark the position of the hands with a little piece of colored tape to indicate where the hands are when the exercise begins. While working, time continually passes by and changes can be observed. This makes children aware that the hands of the clock are moving while time elapses, and it will give a meaning to learning to read the clock. As these weighing exercises are done while sitting behind a table or desk, and because they take some time to do, this is a great opportunity to help children become aware of time, and why learning to read the clock can be useful. When there is more understanding of what is happening, it is likely the child will become more interested in learning. This will give more meaning to timing activities that can be folded in many other exercises as well.

Timing exercises will add more pressure to these exercises, even for adults or older children, as time pressure does have an effect on many people.

It is amazing what time pressure can do to the overall performance of people even though nothing else in the exercise has changed. Time pressure can cause people to make mistakes they would not otherwise make. If they can learn how to deal with pressure while doing these exercises, they will be able to better handle similar situations in real life. Timing is a good way to encourage efficiency and speed without loosing concentration or control. Every time you add more tasks to a sequence, these exercises become more difficult, demanding and challenging. You can easily overload a child, or even an adult, so it is important to keep this in mind and observe carefully how the child reacts.

The next level requires a higher degree of attention from your student and is only suitable for the higher levels. Try this yourself first to know how it feels to do it. Tell a child, or adult, that every time he writes the number 3 (or any other number that needs improvement) he has to write this number very carefully and as perfectly as possible. If necessary have the child practice writing (for example) only 3s first until he is good at it. Another way is to have him write his numbers the  way he is used to, but tell him to have them just touch the line or barely touch it, whichever is suitable. It is fun to look through a magnifying glass to see how close you can get to the line without touching it, as shown by the boy in the picture on the previous page. These writing exercises can be used in many other exercises where documentation is involved as well.

The purpose of choosing only one number first is to not put too much pressure on a child, yet still add another task. You can integrate this writing exercise at an earlier stage if appropriate to the situation. It will give a child a lot of writing practice, and you will notice his handwriting improve because he has to pay more attention to it than he normally would. When ready, more numbers can be added.

Always observe the child very carefully. Even though these exercises appear to be very simple, they can put a lot of pressure on a child if he is not ready.

If necessary, change to another exercise like throwing a Tootie under a leg and catching it or building towers to relieve a child, but go back to the exercise after some time. The most difficult part for the teacher is to judge when to encourage a child to continue or when to deviate to another task for a while. Often, we tend to change tasks too soon without giving a child the chance to really master something. Decisions frequently have to be made on the spot. Learning to struggle and not give up before getting something done is very valuable but we have to be able to judge when it makes sense to continue and when to stop.

The order of adding more difficult sequences to an exercise does not necessarily have to be as indicated above. If, for example, you would like to include the handwriting improvement at an early stage, you can have the child weigh the Tootie and write down the weight without paying attention to the other possibilities. You will have to play with the various ways of sequencing to determine what is important for the child to learn at that moment. It is very important, however, to try to move on as soon as the child is ready, as it is very important to integrate various skills making this exercise as powerful as it is.

It is also possible to integrate math by having a child calculate how many grams he has after adding one Tootie. In this case, have him start with one Tootie and write down the number 1 in the first column. In the second column, he has to write down the weight, and in the third column he writes the total weight, which is in this case, of course, the same. Next, he has to weigh the second Tootie and write down the number in the first column again.

In the second column, he writes down the weight of this Tootie and then calculates how much the total weight is. Now he has to add the two weights and write this in the third column, and so one. In the beginning, you might want to have a child use a calculator to add up the numbers. The next step is to have the child calculate the total in his head first and then check with the calculator to see if he is right. Mark with a red or green pen to indicate if the results are right or wrong.

You can see that Tooties provide a wide variety of learning possibilities. As soon as you, the teacher, the parent, or the therapist, have grasped the concept, there are many ways to use them from the very lowest level up to the highest level suitable of a learning situation. With Tooties, it is possible to be flexible, and adapt to the needs of each child. Children can be very creative as well, and come up with ideas you have never thought of yourself. Any good ideas children suggest should be rewarded, as it means that they are able and willing to be creative. As long as this creativity leads to results, we should encourage children to continue and show what they are able to do. Some children however are

masters at hiding their difficulties and may pretend to be experimenting but they are actually just avoiding what they should do, hiding their weaknesses. We should prevent experimenting when it is used as an escape, as in most cases this attitude does not lead to improvement. It is important to notice children's individual diversion tactics and go back to the level where a child still benefits from repetition and mastery.

Benefits of Tooties for optometrists

By Nathalie Weytjens
Functional Optometrist
Belgium

"He who is unstable in visual space
is insecure in his own ego."
- A.M. Skeffington, O.D. -

"Motility is the seedbed of the mind."
- C. Judson Herrick, Ph. D., Neuro-anatomist -

As a functional optometrist, I frequently use Tooties to develop the visual space world of my patients and myself. I find them very beneficial to motivate my patients after having done the classic visual exercises, such as the use of vectograms and flippers, specific eye movement games and central peripheral exercises, and as a practicing therapist, I also enjoy the fun and the children's enthusiasm. After completing a well-worked out plan of vision exercises that I use from Dr. Baxter Swartwout's' manual and many other ODs such as Sutton, Hendrickson, and Getman, we practice these skills using Tooties, making the exercises more fun and motivating for the patient. Tooties link vision with movement and it is during this time when real learning takes place. Visual skills become more intensively involved when the body is asked to move.

Vision is more than eyesight. How effectively a person is able to see an object depends on how one constructs his visual space world. Tooties compel a person to deal with space and time, balance, movement, bilateral coordination, periphery, listening and speech if you want.

"One does not build a space world by eye-rotations.
It is built by going and doing and feeling and balancing."
- Homer Hendrickson O.D.,
Past President of the OEP Foundation -

This marvelous manual shares many ideas with you on how to use Tooties to improve vision. As the visual space world becomes more organized, something is changed in the behavior of that person and visual skills will show improvement. I believe it occurs in this order and not the other way around.

A Tootie is an object that invites catching, so eye-hand coordination is obviously a skill that is exercised here. But, it is more than that. There is the awareness of yourself when dealing with space and time. Working with Tooties gives one the experience of controlling the body, and of organizing one's movement to solve a problem or to gain perfection.

The following skills are practiced:

1. Eye tracking skills, centering and identification skills
2. Eye-hand coordination skills
3. Symmetry and midline crossing: bilateral organization
4. Laterality and directionality
5. Balance and concentration
6. Visual memory: specific exercises
7. Visual sequential memory: specific exercises
8. Visualization and peripheral vision
9. Figure-ground

To make Tooties more efficient for the development of the visual space, Dr. Hanson, the inventor of Tooties, created many different kinds of Tooties. They can be sorted by color, weight, feeling, sound and size. These combinations provide still more possibilities with which to experiment. Each kind of Tootie provokes a different reaction when patients play with them. They make patients deal with a changing space and time. In addition to the variety of the different types of Tooties, the benefits of the Tootie equipment such as the Toss, the Launcher and the Bounce, make working with Tooties even more fun while exercising vision and the body. Tootie equipment creates new conditions for the mind to solve. This is very good as visual skills are being exercised in circumstances closely related to real life situations. When the visual space world improves, many other things begin to develop, such as self-esteem and body awareness, as well as the ability to concentrate intensely for longer periods of time. The mind becomes more organized, thinking skills improve, and the outside world is less of a threat.

"Vision is an external reflection of an internal,
whole body, neurological organization."
- A.M. Skeffington, O.D. -

Even for the one- and two-year olds, Tooties are very safe to play with and neurologically very stimulating for the eyes with a great variety of different colors and fabric patterns. Other senses are stimulated as well by the use of different weights, sounds and feelings. Compared to blocks children can do a lot more with Tooties and they are safer if the child should step on them or even throw them. However, blocks have the advantage of having different shapes, which is of course also very important for a toddler learning to manipulate.

Large quantities of Tooties provide the best result. While a child is playing with them they move a lot which favors the establishment of a subconsciously felt body image. This can strengthen the integrative capacities of his brain and can reinforce its capacity to code and decode. The development of a sound body image is very important and will later help the child in learning to read and write. Good vision is much more than being able to see clearly, as I mentioned before. Vision is learned and develops through experience. It can be guided and trained to support a child's development when hindrance from the technical revolution and cultural demands inhibit natural development.

Tooties are excellent to help develop math concepts. The visual spacial substance can and should exist before a spoken or written numeral is ever used. The Tootie matrix is designed for this development. Here size and weight are specially studied. The manual also discusses a strong healthy educational philosophy that, if practiced correctly, can bring every human being to succeed in whatever he or she wants.

I believe that all schools, therapy centers and parents with children, can benefit from having Tooties beginning as early as one year old. Tooties are designed to be self-teaching and children will improve their vision automatically. Of course, they will become even better with the right kind of instruction. This manual is great for getting the best results with the Tooties and the Tootie equipment.

It is very valuable for everyone dealing with improving children and adults in any culture. It is not often that a book can be so well thought through that it can be used for many people of different ages.

All children and adults should have regular vision examinations. Even parents of very young children with healthy eyes (between

0 - 3 years) can be given guidance from optometrists about how to give the best care in their child's vision development. The OEP Foundation has two pamphlets, Educators' Guide and Checklist and Parent's Guide and Checklist, with lists of very wise suggestions that can help you to make your child's first few years of life the most meaningful and productive.

Bibliography

Best of Skeffington, Homer Hendrickson, OEP Curriculum 2, Vol. 60, 1987 - 1988 And Vol. 61, 1988 - 1989

Vision, Intelligence and Creativity, Albert A. Sutton, OEP Curriculum 2, Vol. 61, 1988 - 1989

Building a Visual Space World, Albert A. Sutton, OEP Curriculum 2, Vol. 58 Series 2 from 1 to 12

Myopia, Armand R. Bastien, OEP Curriculum 2, Vol. 59, 1986 - 1987 and Vol. 60, 1988

Improving vision with Tooties

By Smita Trivedi BSc (Hons) MCOptom DCLP
Behavioural Optometrist
London, England

"The human being is a SEEING, HEARING,
REMEMBERING, SPEAKING, MOVING organism."
- A. J. Kirshner, OD -

"Sight is what we see with our eyes.
Vision is what we understand with our brain."
- Albert Sutton, OD, MS, FCOVD -

Movement, balance and peripheral awareness are vital elements in any vision therapy program. Movement in space provides a child with stimulation and it awakens the brain. Movement also provides a child with a natural opportunity to actively interact with the environment by integrating and learning from all of what he sees, hears and feels. Therefore, a more meaningful understanding of the environment can develop to support learning.

Tooties have many assets. One of the most important things about them is that they are fun. The fundamental nature of Tooties and the related equipment ensures that movement is involved unless a static activity is planed, such as building. Physical movement promotes interactions with others and with the immediate environment. They are also excellent for organizing because after using them, one can still 'feel' the rhythm and the pattern of movement, and that is learning. You will see how valuable Tooties and the Tootie equipment are in the development of gross motor skills, as well as the development of eye control and cognitive development.

I would like to describe some of the developmental skills important to visual development and to share with you some of the Tooties activities I incorporate at my practice. Many activities can be done to help train the eyes, the body, and to develop vision.

I have only briefly mentioned some of the exercises, as many of them are well described in this comprehensive manual. It is well worth while to consult it for a more detailed description.

Balance

Balance is the foundational skill of all movement. It is the ability to maintain posture and to move the body, under control, in order to learn to coordinate both sides of our bodies. This skill naturally begins with the head, and continues down the body to the shoulders, the trunk, the hips and the legs. Balance is the ability to maintain an upright position so we do not fall down because of gravity and is an important part of running, jumping, standing on one leg, cycling and ball throwing.

Balance is controlled by a combination of three senses: vestibular, vision and proprioception. Vision plays a significant role in balance as approximately 20% of the nerve fibers from the eyes pass through the mid brain (superior colliculous) and interact with the vestibular system.

Activities to develop balance

- A good activity to develop this skill is to walk over a straight line of Tooties with bare feet. The child is immediately aware when he loses his balance which helps him become aware of his own center of gravity, as well as what he must do to maintain balance.
- Another activity is to place a Tootie on any part of the body (head, shoulder, arm, top of the foot) and ask the child to walk from one end of the room to the other. When a Tootie is placed on one of the shoulders that shoulder is weighted down, so an individual naturally begins to make an adjustment to find his own center of gravity. Practicing with the Tootie in this way, a child learns to become aware of the feel for his own center of gravity and he naturally begins to control his bilateral movement patterns in walking. A foundation of bilateralism is established as he becomes aware of balance and becomes better coordinated even without the Tootie.
- A balance board helps train balance. Once the child knows how to maintain his balance on a balance board, he can start to develop a higher level of control by throwing and catching a Tootie while maintaining balance.
- Playing hopscotch and using a Tootie to throw and pick up is another good activity.
- Stand up from a seated position while balancing a Tootie on the head. During this activity it helps to keep the arms folded on the chest while attempting to stand. This is quite an

advanced activity and should only be attempted once balance has been mastered. This activity is also good for improving concentration skills.

Laterality and directionality

Having laterality and directionality is knowing the difference between left and right, forward and backward, and up and down. It is essential in learning where to start to draw letters, where to begin to read on a page, and which side of the word (beginning or end) to begin to read. Bilateral motor skills involve learning to coordinate both sides of the body. It is through balance and posture that we learn to coordinate both sides of our bodies

The human central nervous system is complex. Each child follows an essential sequence of development, progressing from the primitive reflexes to the unique human function of cognition. This organizational sequence begins in utero and progresses vertically through the spinal cord to the level of the midbrain, which develops laterality and the beginning of binocularity, to the level of the cortex (encompasses stereo functions), and finally to the level of the development of complete cortical hemispheric dominance. This is the lateral development where one hemisphere of the cortex becomes the language or dominant hemisphere of the brain, and is the basis of human perceptual abilities. It is only after a child has an understanding of his two sides (laterality) and of his midline that he can know his own position in space and understand an external object's position (directionality).

Activities to develop laterality/directionality

- An activity to help develop laterality and directionality would be to use the Tootie Bounce with a balloon. The balloon moves at a slower speed than a Tootie and enables a child to develop the initial skill of bouncing, as well as tracking. Ask the child to bounce the balloon easily into the air and maintain a rhythm. Gradually introduce bouncing and counting. This makes a cognitive activity which helps build the attention span and an early concept of arithmetic.
- Gradually progress to using the Bounce with a Tootie. The Floaty Tootie can bounce really high and may be better used outdoors. The Tootie Bounce is a great bilateral trainer as the Tooties are constantly crossing the mid-line. Additionally, as

the child holds the Bounce with both hands symmetry will be enhanced.

- Arrange a situation where a child can throw Tooties to different colored piles. First throw a designated number using one hand, then throw the same amount with the other hand. Finally, alternate hands so the child has to cross his own midline.

Peripheral awareness

Peripheral awareness is connected to balance and movement. It tells us about spatial relationships, depth perception and movement. The perceptual organization of information that enters through one's senses begins with awareness of sensory information at the periphery. This organization gradually increases in meaning as it approaches the center. Therefore the central peripheral relationship is dependent on movement and balance.

Activities to develop peripheral awareness

- Walk on a walking rail or maintain balance on a board in a stable balance position and catch a Tootie thrown from the periphery.
- Bounce on a trampoline and catch a Tootie thrown from the periphery.
- Perform Kirschner arrows, Hart Chart saccades or walking rail activities while using peripheral vision to avoid Tooties thrown by the therapist. Begin by throwing Tooties in a regular rhythm, then, gradually introduce throwing in an irregular fashion.
- All of the above are also great activities for sport vision therapy.
- Place one Tootie on the floor at a preconceived center. Then, either in a circular or a rectangular manner form spirals, or shape a large labyrinth around the central Tootie. Work on seeing the center Tootie as well as the Tooties at the outer peripheral spiral or labyrinth, depending on what you build.

Visual-motor coordination

Visual-motor coordination is the ability to coordinate vision with movement. This is important in the classroom because it helps a child to copy things, write, color and cut things properly (fine motor skills). It also helps a child to track when reading and to line up letters and/or numbers in columns and rows.

Good tracking skills allow us to follow a line of print without losing our place. It is our oculomotor system that lets us accurately direct our eye movements. With our mind we learn to control these eye movement skills. There are three main types of oculomotor skills: fixation (maintain steady visual attention on a target), saccades (quick and accurate eye jumps from one target to another) and pursuits (smoothly follow a moving target).

A strong integration between our central and peripheral vision systems is critical to good reading skills. Our peripheral vision allows us locate objects and process where they are in space, but our clear, central vision tells us what it is we are looking at.

These two systems are sometimes referred to as the "Where is it?" and "What is it?" systems. In reading, our central vision processes the letters, while our peripheral vision locates the next word and tells us where to aim our eyes next. If there is not continuous simultaneous processing between these two systems, reading will be jerky and a loss of place will be common resulting in inadequate fluidity and comprehension.

Activities to improve tracking skills (oculomotor function)

- Make a straight line of Tooties on the floor. Ask the child to lie on his back with the shoulders on the Tooties and roll from one end of the Tooties line to the other (from left to right and right to left). This improves orientation skills as it requires coordination between the eyes and the body to keep the body rolling in a straight line. In addition left-right and right-left fixation, pursuits, and saccades are practiced. Once the task of rolling in a straight line with the aid of the Tooties has been mastered, the Tooties are removed and the child should still be able to roll in a straight line.
- Start with the Tootie Bounce and a balloon. Large balloons move very slowly and allow a child to track and focus accurately. As the child improves, make smaller and smaller balloons by putting in less air. Progress to a Tootie Bounce using a Classic Tootie (151 grams), as this is the easiest. Follow with a Tweenie (100 grams) and later, a Floaty (75 grams) both of which are harder because of their bouncing features. Developmental progression is important. It is important to observe and accept each child's level of ability and only gradually increase the level of difficulty.

- Introduce the Tootie Launcher when the child is ready. Start with a red Tootie on one end and have a child jump or stamp his foot on the other end. Do not tell him to catch, just observe to see if he tries. If he shows no signs of catching then you need to try one of the above activities first. Repeat until he can do it consistently. Then move the red Tootie down slightly so a green Tootie can fit on the end. When the child can catch two consistently, advance to three Tooties with a yellow Tootie at the end. It is very important to maintain the sequence of the Tooties. The new Tootie always goes at the end.
  After yellow comes blue, and later, any other different color can be chosen. Write the sequence down with number one being the red Tootie and place the paper face down. The child replaces the Tooties by memory and can turn the paper over to verify, if necessary. See the section on Visual memory later. Most children can catch their age in Tooties after several hours of practice. After five Tooties suggest that the child overlap the Tooties if desired. For more detailed information and more exercises please check the Launcher chapter.
- Finally use the Tootie Toss. This is the large net you throw the Tootie against, and it returns quickly to you. Encourage the child to throw but do not mention catching. As the child becomes more proficient using the Tootie Launcher and Toss ask the child to alternate throwing hands which increases the demand. This will also mean that the child will be reaching across his body to catch the Tootie. The ability to bilaterally reach across the body's midline is an important developmental milestone.

Activities to develop eye/hand coordination and depth perception:

- Throw a Tootie up and catch it with both hands. Try to make the two sides of your body move symmetrically. After this is mastered, throw a Tootie up so it just touches the ceiling, and catch it with both hands. When this is mastered, throw the Tootie up as close to ceiling as you can without touching it, and catch with both hands. Finally, throw the Tootie up as close to the ceiling without touching, but this time, let the Tootie get as close to the floor before catching it with both hands.
- Repeat all of the above while throwing and catching with the right hand, then left hand. Keep your eyes on the Tootie during the entire activity.

- Repeat all of the above, but this time throwing with the right hand and catching with left hand, and then throwing with the left hand and catching with right hand.
- Once an individual can do all of the above, use two Tooties (one in each hand) and throw and catch two Tooties simultaneously. If different weights are used, catch the lightest one with the right hand and the heaviest one with the left hand, and vice versa.
- Try to throw and catch a Tootie/Tooties with your eyes closed.
- Create your own way of throwing and catching.

Focusing skills

Focusing skills allow us to see clearly, especially up close. At the close ranges required for reading, focusing skills need to maintain clear sharp images for extended periods of time. Near-far focus skills include the ability to quickly shift focus when looking from near to far, such as when children have to look from their desks to the board at school or when children are playing with others outside or in a gym. The Tootie Toss is especially useful for this exercise.

Activities to develop focusing skills

- The Tootie Toss is helpful to develop this skill. Use different hands for throwing and catching, and use different types of Tooties. Classic Tooties weigh about 151 grams or one third of a pound. Lighter Tooties like the Tweenie, 100 grams, and the Floaty, 45 grams, are more difficult. The most difficult ones of the 'special' Tooties are those where the center of gravity is not in the center, but near one end, and the weight shifts from time to time.
- Change the angle of the Toss by flipping it upside down. When both the long and short legs are touching the floor the Tootie returns higher and slower than when only the long leg is touching the floor.
- Change the distance of the Toss. For little children about the ages of 1 to 5 years, it is best to have them sit on the floor cross legged with their back to a wall. Put a number of Tooties in their lap and ask them to throw. Do not tell them to catch. Normally the Tootie will return at about chest level and they will grasp it when it has stopped. That is considered a catch. This is the lowest level of catching.

It is amazing that many older children will start to catch the same way. Later, they should be able to catch away from their body with two hands, and later with either hand. As they become more confident, move the Toss further away. Consider changing the angle of the Toss to make it easier for them in the beginning. It depends on how a child throws, but the goal is to have the Tootie return at about chest level.

- When the Tootie Toss is very close to the child they love to throw and catch with their eyes closed. In this way you can see what is happening to information as the brain processes it in a non visual way. This is called proprioception, where the child adjusts the power and angle of his throw in order to be successful. He also knows when he threw it so he has an idea when and where it should return.

Eye teaming skills

Eye teaming skills control how we use and aim our eyes together, and is an important skill that keeps us from seeing double. The ability to use both eyes as a 'team', or single functioning pair, is what allows our brain to fuse the two separate pictures coming in from each eye into a single image. This skill is called binocularity.

Activities to develop binocular vision

- Build igloos. Start with a round circle of Tooties about 15 to 18 inches in diameter. This takes about 15 Tooties. Add another layer but do not tell the child that the joints should be overlapped as when laying bricks. Let the child discover this. Each layer should come in a little closer until the igloo is finally closed at the top. Now hold the child's hands so he can sit on the igloo. If it holds, then ask him to lift his legs so his full weight is on the igloo. If it collapses tell him now he gets to build another and even better one. Children love the feeling when it collapses.
- A more advanced stage that incorporates math in a fun way is to have a child record the number of Tooties in each layer on paper. Later, record the weight of all the Tooties in each layer so they can calculate the total number of Tooties in their igloo and the total weight.
- Monocular fixation in a binocular field (MFBF) is a link to simultaneous perception or binocularity which is the first level of sensory fusion. The child wears red-green glasses and

looks at a selection of red and green Tooties which he has to pick out scattered on the floor. Suppression of one eye or the other results in the disappearance of the opposing color Tooties.

Visual perception skills

Visual perception skills are needed to understand, analyze, and interpret what we see. Visual discrimination lets us see the differences between objects that are similar. Good visual discrimination helps keep us from getting confused, for example, when we read. It is visual discrimination that lets us see that 'was' and 'saw' are different even though they have the same letters.

Activities to enhance perceptual skills

- Ask the child to sort a pile of Tooties. At first the child will sort by colors.
- As children play with the Tooties more, they will start sorting in different weights. Continue until they are aware of JNDs (just noticeable differences). The highest level attainable is when anyone can discriminate 5 gram differences. Very few people can do this, so in general use the Metric Weight Set where 12 Tooties are each 10 grams different going from 70 to 180 grams.

Visual memory

Visual memory is another important perceptual skill. It helps us recall what we have seen, and visual sequential memory is important in reading. As mentioned above, the Tootie Launcher is one of the best activities for visual memory and sequencing.

Activity to develop visual memory

- Show a child about 10 to 20 different Tooties and give him time to look for one minute. Then cover them up and ask the child to recall the Tooties. This can also be fun for younger children when the number of Tooties is reduced in number to two, and gradually increased as the child becomes proficient.

Activities to develop visual sequential memory

- Place two or three Tooties in a row. Then cover them up and ask the child to recall the sequence. Gradually increase the number of Tooties.

- Using the Launcher is a fun way and also incorporates movement. Start with the red Tootie and then introduce green, yellow and blue. Maintain this initial sequence and afterwards let the child make their own choice of color. The new Tootie always goes on the eye at the end of the Launcher.

Figure ground

Figure ground is the perceptual skill that lets us pick out details without getting confused by the background or surrounding images. This skill is especially helpful when we are presented with a lot of visual information at one time. To emphasize the importance of contrast, place the Tootie Toss against a dark background and use a dark Tootie. This can be very difficult so a light colored Tootie should be used.

Activities to develop figure ground

- Have lots of Tooties scattered on the floor and ask the child to find a particular Tootie. Use only two identical Tooties, one you show the child and the other is in the pile of scattered Tooties.
- Later use two Smoothy or Floaty Tooties. These could be different colors so now the child has to feel each one to be able to find the one that matches.

Visual closure

Visual closure is the ability to visualize a complete whole when given incomplete information or a partial picture. This skill helps us understand things quickly because our visual system does not have to process every detail to recognize what we are seeing. When we are reading, this skill helps us recognize sight words.

Activity to work on visual closure

- Make a shape with Tooties but leave gaps so the child has to work out what it is.

Visual form constancy

Visual form constancy is the ability to mentally turn and rotate objects in our minds and picture what they would look like. This skill helps us distinguish differences in size, shape and orientation. Children with poor form constancy may frequently reverse letters and numbers.

Activity to work on form constancy

- Have a child make a triangle, rectangle or some other shape out of Tooties. Then make identical ones turned on their side or upside down, or make them smaller or larger.

Using the Tooties to remediate a child's balance insufficiency, his inability to cross the midline, or his inability to pursue, fixate on or track an object will help the child's learning and impact on his success in the classroom. Make the Tootie activity relevant to each individual child and their developmental stage. Be creative and you have the recipe for successful learning!

Case Study: Jaydine (aged 10)

I have chosen Jaydine as a case study to illustrate the benefits of Tooties in the process of vision improvement. Jaydine and her mum were referred by a Special Education Needs teacher (SEN) in April 2004. Jaydine was in year 4 of Primary School and had been assessed by the school as having special needs and whose standard of work was below average. According to her teacher, Jaydine worked really hard and to her 'maximum capacity' but struggled with her reading, writing and numeracy tasks.

Background

Jaydine was born in England. At the age of 3 she moved to Jamaica to live with her grandparents and returned to live in England at the age of 7. While in Jamaica she was achieving high grades (As/Bs) and could recite her times tables up to 4. On returning to school here in the UK, she found learning her tables difficult as it was taught differently to the method she had been used to.

Vision Analysis

The vision testing revealed a severely reduced functional field of vision and Jaydine could only see hand movements. Her visual acuity has improved tremendously to 6/6 R and L with plano 2 prism based down yoked prism lenses.

Further testing revealed she had inadequate eye movements, accommodation and binocular vision. Vision information processing tests indicated difficulties with laterality, directionality, visual perceptual skills and visual motor integration.

Jaydine continued with lenses for a year and a half and there was some improvement in her functional field of vision. Her mother noticed an improvement in Jaydine's schoolwork and also her confidence. However, without the spectacles her visual acuities reverted back to hand movements only R and L.

Vision training with Tooties was recommended and started in December 2005. Jaydine, aged 10, was seen once a week for a three-hour session for five weeks with my daughter, aged 15. Often, when working with Tooties, a young enthusiastic person of a similar age to the patient can work exceptionally well with them. Her field of vision improved and her confidence increased. I then continued to see Jaydine for three hours on a weekly basis for a further five weeks.

In February, 2006, there was a great improvement in all her visual perceptual skills except her visual memory and visual sequential memory skills. Further Tootie sessions were continued for an hour on a bi-weekly basis. In May 2006 a reflex program was advised and started.

Jaydine's confidence has improved enormously and she no longer needs her yoked prism lenses. Her visual acuities are 6/6 R and L without spectacles and she has a full functional field of vision. In September, 2006, Jaydine started secondary school, starting year 7. Without the help of the Tooties the transition would have been a huge obstacle, but with the help of the Tooties it has been made in to a smooth transition from Primary to Secondary school.

Jaydine and her mum's comments follow:

Jaydine (own words): *"The Tooties have helped me a lot in so many ways. The Tooties have helped me to open my vision and make me see more. Because of the Tooties I can see so much I could not see before. Tooties have helped me to concentrate more on what I am doing."*

Jaydine's mother wrote the following letter: *"I write further to recent conversation and outline below the benefits upon which the Tooties have had on Jaydine."*

- *Her vision has improved remarkably. She no longer wears spectacles.*
- *There is an improvement in her balance and co-ordination. She appears less clumsy.*

- *She can carry out given tasks more methodically.*
- *Her confidence has improved. She is less shy. She no longer regresses and has a better relationship with her peers.*
- *She expresses her opinions more freely.*
- *She has made improvement in her school work.*
- *With the aid of Tooties, Jaydine's vision and personality have changed for the better. She enjoyed the use of Tooties because she was learning/improving through play.*
- *Prior to the use of the Tooties I thought that Jaydine had special educational needs.*

Other Tootie testimonials

Harry (own words): *"It has made my math better when I learned to weigh the Tooties. It has made my catching better and co-ordination. It has improved my science. I think I can concentrate better and I feel more confident about my writing. It was hard at times but then I got better."*

Harry's mother wrote: *"Since Harry undertook the Tooties program we have noticed a marked improvement in the following areas:"*

- *Overall confidence, and in particular in social situations*
- *His ability to undertake tasks such as homework more independently.*
- *His speed and accuracy of reading.*
- *His ability to read for longer periods of time independently and for pleasure.*
- *While Tooties work on a number on levels to overcome the difficulties posed by my son's dyspraxia, the fact that it is seen by him as fun with an emphasis on reward and progress it is a much more attractive way of working.*

Marion is a special needs teacher who attended a Tooties workshop in London and now uses Tooties. Her comments:

"Tooties are wonderful! Thank you for introducing me to Tooties. An opportunity to enhance learning skills and really enjoyed the experience - in fact, learning sneaks up on those lucky enough to share the Tooties experience. As an example, a group of 10 children with various speaking and listening difficulties were able to share a description of a single Tootie for three rounds. Each child, each time, had to contribute a new observation describing the Tootie. The sense of achievement was great. Without doubt children who are finding their confidence shaken by lack of

academic achievement are encouraged as they themselves realize that they can count, sort, build, balance, catch, and open their imagination."

- *Yes, they have success.*
- *Yes, they want to join in and take part.*
- *Yes, they feel more confident in tackling new experiences.*
- *Yes, Tooties are wonderful.*

Conclusions

Dear Reader,

With this manual I hope to have offered you a wide choice of practical exercises to help children develop their self-generated learning abilities. Training courses can be arranged and are available to those who want to understand more extensive ways to use the materials. Please check the back of the book for useful contacts. It cannot be emphasized enough that children should be allowed to learn how to learn by themselves and develop their problem-solving skills through the integrated use of body and mind. The more the body is developed with a solid, skillful and independently functioning foundation, the more the mind can be free to be creative and be enthusiastic about learning new things. The child now instinctively knows that when he wants to learn something new, he has the refined skills to be successful.

It is important to guide children, especially very young children, towards the sensible use of electronic equipment and reduce the overload of electronically-generated images and sounds from televisions, computer games, DVDs and MP3 players, as well as computers and other electronic game devices. A growing, young sensory system needs and benefits from interactive physical activities in a real world to become fine-tuned in a natural way. This is the way children learn to distinguish and to integrate a wide variety of sensations and motor skills, including important visual motor skills. And, it has a significant influence on the ability to better distinguish and perform on an abstract and emotional level later in life. Ideally young children should not watch TV or play computer games at all, as it can disrupt and ruin their natural capability to create their own fantasy play and develop their individual creativity and imagination, not to mention the negative impact it can have on the development of the neural system. There are several books on the effect electronic equipment has on young children. Consult the list of recommended literature at the back of the book to learn more about the influence of watching television.

Up to date scientific evidence shows how watching TV can slow down the body's metabolic rate, can stunt the development of children's brains, and increase the likelihood of children developing ADHD and other developmental delays.

Providing children with a wide variety of experiences also applies to the kinds of toys we offer. In order to develop and refine the sensory system it is important to provide children with a variety of materials to play with. Paper, wood, metal, fabrics, plastic, as well as materials found in the woods or in gardens provide a wide assortment of manipulative experiences. Every single material has a different texture, weight, color, sound, or other feature providing children with an abundance of sensory input which is important for development and learning. Ideally, toys should not be ready made, as this leaves children with very little room for their own creativity and imagination. Provide children with beneficial, worthwhile toys which allow for building and experimentation and give them the learning opportunities they need to develop to their fullest potential. In addition, give children small tasks in and around the house and gradually let them help with bigger or more complicated tasks. This helps them to better understand every day life and how to participate in it, adding to their wide range of experiences and practical knowledge.

Children have to first learn to master, understand and deal with the 'real world' and to develop their motor skills, including visual motor skills together with their self-generated learning abilities as described in this manual. Except for some extremely talented people, skills can only be mastered through movement, meaningful and creative play, and intensive practice. The same holds true for sports and music. If a person wants to become a good piano player, daily practice is essential. After a certain level of competency has been achieved, practice is necessary to maintain the skill. The same applies to the learning skills needed in school and every day life.

After learning to live in the 'real world' children will have become well equipped and talented enough to gradually start learning to deal with the digital and virtual world.

A child needs good judgement to be able to 'survive' in the digital world where things or people can prove to be quite different or even more dangerous than they may appear. I have observed eight- and nine-year-old children who seemed to have already escaped into the virtual world because the real world appeared to be too difficult to handle. Many of these children have not learned to understand and to deal with problem solving. They avoid playing with friends and become socially isolated as well. Basic skills, which are easier to learn early in life, then have to be mastered at a late time, when other children of the same age have moved on to higher levels.

When children are able to develop activities and experiences that activate the body, they will be tired enough in the evening to (want to) go to sleep and rest. The real and meaningful experiences of the day can be digested, sleep is refreshing, and the child can wake up with renewed energy for the new day. The same applies to adults. Even though Tooties are excellent for development, children should be provided with a variety of experiences and challenges as long as they help children develop their (learning) skills and provide them with understandable feedback. Learning to skip, juggle, or play hopscotch are just some of the many activities that should be reintroduced into the every day lives of children. These activities may seem old fashioned but they provide children with many, extremely important learning opportunities, as long as we encourage children to explore and not tell them exactly what to do and how to do it.

What could there be to explore about skipping? There are many different ways to do it. Why don't you experiment together with some children and see how many different ways you can discover.

Do not forget that parents and caregivers make a big impact on a child's development. Slowing down our tempo, good planning, and good quality time provide just part of the healthy foundation only we can give to our children. Take the time to learn the skill of observation and train the ability to 'slip into someone else's shoes' and look at behavior from another perspective. Granted, it takes time, practice, and acceptance of errors we ourselves may make. It is the same acceptance and understanding we want to give our children when they make 'errors'.

We all learn from errors or 'mistakes', and having a healthy attitude about them allows ourselves and our children to grow with a positive attitude they will be able to take with them as they grow older.

I hope to have inspired you with my view on development and self-generated learning abilities. By sharing my experiences and the techniques I learned from Dr. John Hanson with you, I hope more children will be able to develop to their full potential.

Tooties are truly wonderful.

Thea van Eijk-Looijmans

Recommended Resources

In this section resources are listed for those interested in further study. It is not intended as a full resource reference for information printed in this book. Some of the literature (* starred) is intended for the professional or highly motivated parent who is interested in a more extended foundation.

Ayres, A. Jean. 1989. *Sensory Integration and the Child*. Los Angeles, California: Western Psychological Services, ISBN 0-87424-158-8. (*)

Bell, Nanci. 1986. *Visualizing and Verbalizing For Language Comprehension and Thinking*, Revised Edition, San Luis Obispo, California: Gander Publishing, ISBN 0-945-856-01-6. (*)

Bell, Nanci. 1997. *Seeing Stars: Symbol Imagery for Phonemic Awareness, Sight Words and Spelling*. San Luis Obispo, California: Gander Publishing, ISBN 0-945-856-06-7. (*)

Berne, Samuel A. 2002. *Without Ritalin*. Chicago, Illinois: Keats Publishing (McGraw-Hill), ISBN 0-658-01215-0.

Cleveland, Alexandra, B. Caton, L. Adler. 1994. *Activities Unlimited: Creative and Exciting Sensory Motor Activities*. Elgin, Illinois: Building Blocks, ISBN 0-943452-17-1.

Cook, David, *When Your Child Struggles The Myths of 20/20 Vision: What Every Parent Needs to Know*, ISBN 0-9632657-0-9

Eide, Brock, F. Eide. 2006. *The Mislabeled Child*. New York: Hyperion, ISBN 1-4013-0225-4.

Getman, Gerald N. 1993. *How to Develop your Child's Intelligence*. Santa Ana, California: Optometric Extension Program, ISBN 0-979780-05-1.

Getman, Gerald N. 1992. *Smart in everything .... except school*, Santa Ana, California: Vision Extension, ISBN 0-929780-03-5

Goddard, Sally, 2005. *Reflexes, Learning and Behavior: A Window into the Child's Mind*. Eugene, Oregon: Fern Ridge Press, ISBN 0-9764543-0-0. (*)

Goddard, Sally. 2004. *The Well Balanced Child: Movement and Early Learning*, Stroud, Gloucestershire, UK: Hawthorn Press, ISBN 978-1-903458-63-1.

Hall, Susan L., Moats, L.C. 1999. *Straight Talk about Reading*, Chicago, Illinois: Contemporary Books, ISBN 0-8092-2857-2.

Healy, Jane M. 1987. *Your Child's Growing Mind: A Practical guide to Brain Development and Learning From Birth to Adolescence*. New York: Doubleday, ISBN 0-385-46930-6.

Healy, Jane M. 1990. *Endangered Minds: Why Children Don't Think and What We Can Do About It*. New York: Simon & Schuster, ISBN 0-684-85620-4.

McCall, Renée M., D. H. Craft. 2000. *Moving With A Purpose: Developing Programs for Preschoolers of All Abilities*, Champaign, Illinois: Human Kinetics, ISBN 0-88011-976-4.

Sher, Barbara. 1997. *Moving Right Along*, Hugo, Minnesota: PDP Press, ISBN 0-930681-03-7.

Sigman, Aric. 2005. *Remotely Controlled; How television is damaging our lives*, London: Vermillion, ISBN 978-0-09-190690-0

Sunbeck, Deborah. 1996. *Infinity Walk*, Torrance, California: Jalmar Press, ISBN 1-880396-31-9.

www.oepf.org website of Optometric Extension Program Foundation USA with general information about vision and store with books for parents and professionals

www.soe-optometry.org/ website of The European Society of Optometry (SOE)

Tootie Launcher

Score Card   For free digital score cards mail to: info@spelenmoet.nl

Attempt	Goal	Number caught	% caught	Lap time	Decimal time	Past time	1	2	3	4	5	6	7	8	9 colors caught	10	11	12	13	14	15	16	17
1																							
2																							
3																							
4																							
5																							
6																							
7																							
8																							
9																							
10																							
11																							
12																							
13																							
14																							
15																							
16																							
17																							
18																							
19																							
20																							
21																							
22																							
23																							
24																							
25																							
26																							
27																							
28																							
29																							
30																							

Tootie Launcher

Score Card For free digital score cards mail to: info@spelenmoet.nl

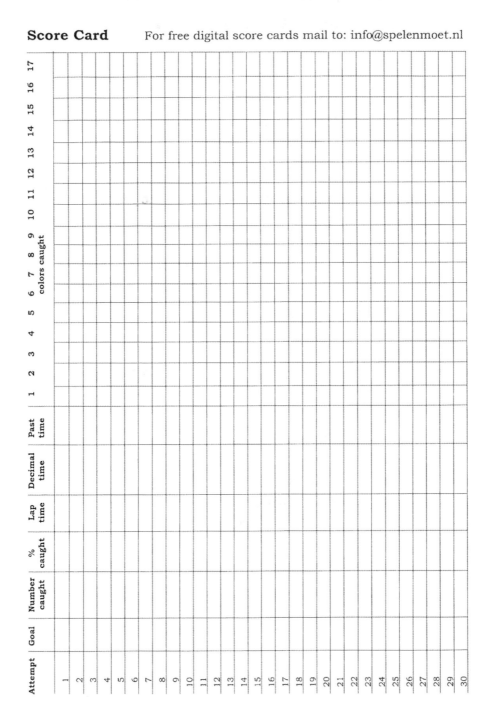

Behavioral Vision Care contact information

Optometric Extension Program Foundation

1921 E. Carnegie Ave., Suite 3-L
Santa Ana, CA 92705-5510

Telephone	949-250-8070
Fax	949-250-8157
Website	www.oepf.org
E-mail	oep@oepf.org

College of Optometrists in Vision Development

215 West Garfield Road, Suite 200
Aurora, OH 44202

Telephone	330-995-0718 | 888-268-3770
Fax	330-995-0719
Website	www.covd.org
E-mail	info@covd.org

Neuro-Optometric Rehabilitation Association, International, Inc.

P.O. Box 14934
Irvine, CA 92623-4934

Telephone	866 2C-BETTR (866-222-3887)
Fax	949-250-8157
Website	www.nora.cc
E-mail	aiko.heard@nora.cc

Spelen Moet !

Thea van Eijk-Looijmans
Jan Tooropstraat 8
5642 AK Eindhoven
The Netherlands
Telephone   +31 (0)40 2815696
Fax   +31 (0)40 7871477
E-mail   info@spelenmoet.nl (Dutch)
Website   www.spelenmoet.nl (Dutch)
E-mail   office@tootieseurope.com (English)
Website   www.tootieseurope.com (English)

Austria

Tooties Austria
Sieben Sinne
N.Lechner
A-1030 Wien
Telephone/fax: +43-01-718 83 83
E-mail   office@tooties.at
Website   www.tooties.at

UK

Smita Trivedi BSc (Hons) MCOptom DCLP
Behavioural Optometrist
Cleveden House
455 High Road
Wood Green
London N22 8JD
England
Telephone   +44 (0)208 889 0818
Fax   +44 (0)208 888 0399
E-mail   smita@smitatrivedi.com
Website   www.smitatrivedi.com

Tooties International USA

Website   www.tooties.com
E-mail   info@tooties.com

Learning to Learn

How to use Tooties
to teach basic learning skills and
self-generated learning abilities
through movement

Thea van Eijk-Looijmans

Optometric Extension Program
Foundation

The OEP Foundation, founded in 1928, is an international non-profit organization dedicated to continuing education and re-search for the advancement of human progress through education in behavioral vision care.
OEP Foundation, Inc.
1921 E. Carnegie Ave., Suite 3-L
Santa Ana, CA 92705
www.oepf.org
Managing editor: Sally Marshall Corngold

Library of Congress Cataloging-in-Publication Data
Van Eijk-Looijmans, Thea.
   Learning to learn : how to use tooties to teach basic learning skills and self-generated learning abilities through movement / Thea van Eijk-Looijmans. -- [2nd ed.].
      p. cm.
   Originally published by Spelen Moet!, The Netherlands.
   Includes bibliographical references.
   ISBN 978-0-929780-26-9
   1. Movement education. 2. Movement, Psychology of. 3. Brain stimulation. 4. Academic achievement. I. Title.
   GV452.V36 2010
   372.86'8--dc22

                          2010003108

                ****

Optometry is the health care profession specifically licensed by state law to prescribe lenses, optical devices and procedures to improve human vision. Optometry has advanced vision therapy as a unique treatment modality for the development and remediation of the visual process. Effective vision therapy requires extensive understanding of:
- the effects of lenses (including prisms, filters and occlud-ers)
- the variety of responses to the changes produced by lenses
- the various physiological aspects of the visual process
- the pervasive nature of the visual process in human behav-ior

As a consequence, effective vision therapy requires the supervi-sion, direction and active involvement of the optometrist.
                ****

Originally published by Spelen Moet!, The Netherlands
ISBN/EAN 978-90-812260-1-1
NUR 840